BRITAIN IN OLD PHOTOGRAPHS

THE ROYAL
NORFOLK REGIMENT

The gateway to Britannia Barracks, *c.* 1879. The view beyond shows the city of Norwich. Over the years, thousands of men from the city and country have passed through this gateway on their way to join their county regiment.

BRITAIN IN OLD PHOTOGRAPHS

THE ROYAL
NORFOLK REGIMENT

NEIL R. STOREY

SUTTON PUBLISHING LIMITED

Sutton Publishing Limited
Phoenix Mill · Thrupp · Stroud
Gloucestershire · GL5 2BU

First published 1997

Cover photographs: *title page*: boy soldiers of the
2nd Battalion, Aldershot, *c*. 1930; *half title page*:
Captain A.H. Luard (centre), the officers and
colour-sergeants of A Company, 2nd Battalion,
Norfolk Regiment, Aldershot, *c*. 1895.

British Library Cataloguing in Publication Data
A catalogue record for this book is available from the
British Library.

ISBN 0-7509-1456-4

Typeset in 10/12 Perpetua.
Typesetting and origination by
Sutton Publishing Limited.
Printed in Great Britain by
Ebenezer Baylis, Worcester.

THIS BOOK IS DEDICATED TO

The memory of my great-grandfather Frederick
Griffin 5th Battalion, Norfolk Regiment 1914–18.

My friend and mentor Captain John Lincoln MC
1st Battalion, Royal Norfolk Regiment 1944–5.

And all who served with pride under the badge of Britannia, especially 'Doogie', 'Gilly' and 'Strips'.

CONTENTS

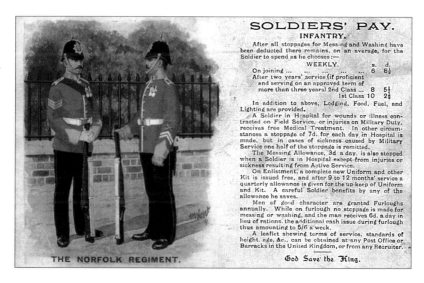

THE NORFOLK REGIMENT.

SOLDIERS' PAY.

INFANTRY.

After all stoppages for Messing and Washing have been deducted there remains, on an average, for the Soldier to spend as he chooses:—

WEEKLY.   s.   d.

On joining 6   8½

After two years' service (if proficient and serving on an approved term of more than three years) 2nd Class ... 8   5½

                     1st Class 10   2½

In addition to above, Lodging, Food, Fuel, and Lighting are provided.

A Soldier in Hospital for wounds or illness contracted on Field Service, or injuries on Military Duty, receives free Medical Treatment. In other circumstances a stoppage of 7d. for each day in Hospital is made, but in cases of sickness caused by Military Service one half of the stoppage is remitted.

The Messing Allowance, 3d. a day, is also stopped when a Soldier is in Hospital except from injuries or sickness resulting from Active Service.

On Enlistment, a complete new Uniform and other Kit is issued free, and after 9 to 12 months' service a quarterly allowance is given for the up-keep of Uniform and Kit. A careful Soldier benefits by any of the allowance he saves.

Men of good character are granted Furloughs annually. While on furlough no stoppage is made for messing or washing, and the man receives 6d. a day in lieu of rations, the additional cash issue during furlough thus amounting to 5/6 a week.

A leaflet shewing terms of service, standards of height, age, &c., can be obtained at any Post Office or Barracks in the United Kingdom, or from any Recruiter.

God Save the King.

INTRODUCTION

King Charles II was responsible for the formation of the British Standing Army and before his death had raised five regiments of infantry. His successor, James II, because of the opposition to him as king compounded in the Monmouth Rebellion, raised another five regiments. Among them in 1685 was Colonel Henry Cornwall's Regiment, the most distant ancestor of the Royal Norfolk Regiment. Although not to see action in the Monmouth Rebellion the regiment was despatched to fight in Ireland at the Boyne and Aughrim and thence to serve in Portugal in the War of Spanish Succession under the Duke of Marlborough. During this war the regiment's outstanding bravery, steadfastness and example at the Battle of Almanza in 1707 caused Queen Anne to bestow on them the 'Figure of Britannia' to be worn as a badge and to be emblazoned on the colours of the regiment. This honour was proudly worn by all battalions for 250 years. When the command of the army moved from royal to ministerial rule and the army was reorganised from Colonels' Regiments to numbered regiments of foot in the mid-eighteenth century, Colonel Cornwall's Regiment became the 9th Foot. In 1761 the 9th were part of the expedition to Belle Isle, an island on the French coast in the Bay of Biscay. The regiment distinguished themselves at the landing and they earned their first battle honour when the French capitulated.

In 1775 the 9th was sent to fight in the American War of Independence and maintained the regiment's reputation in a number of engagements, notably the battles of Three Rivers and Fort St Anne. Unfortunately the 9th was part of General 'Gentleman Johnny' Burgoyne's force captured at Saratoga and its men were made prisoners of war for the next four years. The colours of the regiment were not captured, however, thanks to Lieutenant-Colonel Hill who tore them from their poles and secreted them in his luggage for the duration of his imprisonment. On his return they were presented to the king and eventually laid up in the Chapel of the Royal Military Academy at Sandhurst where they may be seen today – the oldest extant colours of the British Army.

It was not until 1781 when the bedraggled ex-prisoners returned from the Americas, but in the meantime the regiment had to be reinstated. The Earl of Ligonier, colonel of the regiment, brought his men to Norfolk to reconstitute its numbers. Recruiting in those days was often a thankless task; a recruiting party would consist of an officer, recruiting sergeant, two men and a drummer and had to compete with the stigma of drunkenness and violence associated with a soldier's life. Drummers would have the shillings on their beating drum: the shilling, a day's pay, would be collected by the soldier on enlistment, remembering that in those days, enlistment was for life. It was not unknown for men

Colour-Sergeant and Ensign with colour of the 9th (East Norfolk) Regiment from a painting by Charles Hamilton-Smith, *c.* 1813.

under sentence of death to obtain a pardon by enlisting and serving in the army. Very determined efforts were made with the cooperation of local nobility, gentry, clergy and inhabitants, and the sum of £6,599 11s 6d was raised in two days from which 3 guineas were given to every newly joined recruit. It was not long before the regiment was returned to full strength. At this time the War Office decided, for the first time, to associate some regiments with English counties; each colonel of the regiment involved was asked to make his choice. So impressed was the Earl of Ligonier with the help and hospitality of the people of Norwich and with so many men of the county swelling its ranks at the time, he asked that the 9th be associated with Norfolk. In 1782 they were accorded the title of the 9th (East Norfolk) Regiment.

Following a few years in England and a peaceful tour of Ireland the 9th was sent to the French West Indies in 1788 during the French Revolutionary Wars. Although dubbed a 'white man's grave' the battle casualties were relatively light but the regiment was cut down, however, by yellow fever and other tropical diseases, returning to Norwich in 1796, 'a pathetic wreck of a regiment'. Re-established with recruits from across the region it was a true East Anglian regiment which proceeded to the Peninsula and served in the campaigns under the Duke of Wellington. Hard fighting throughout by the 9th earned nine battle honours, notably Rolica, Busaco and Corunna. This last action was the withdrawal during the depths of the winter in 1808. The 9th was in the force under overall command of Sir John Moore, providing the rearguard to enable the embarkation at Corunna. Sir John was shot from his horse in the ensuing battle, carried from the battlefield by the men of the 9th and he was buried by them under fire, 'darkly at the dead of night'. To mark this event the 'black worm' of silk was embroidered into the drummers' and officers' shoulder straps of their full dress uniforms and the black backing to the badges, worn more recently, mourns Sir John.

Further battles for the 9th were fought in Spain and Portugal. During this campaign the Figure of Britannia on their uniforms and colours was mistaken for the Virgin Mary, and the entire regiment were believed to be 'holy men'. This title rapidly spread and the nickname of the 'Holy Boys' has stuck for over 250 years.

In the early part of the nineteenth century the 9th were sent to India, a country eventually to become a familiar station for the regiment over the years. Battle honours such as Cabool in 1842, earned for their storming of the Khyber Pass in the First Afghan War, were rapidly awarded; more followed in the First Sikh War at Moodkee and after the 150-mile march in blistering heat completed in six days prior to the Battle of Ferozeshalir.

Following the regiment's service in the Crimean War, where they took part in the Siege of Sebastopol in 1854, the regiment was stationed in Gibraltar, the Cape, and took part in a unique tour of China and Japan. It was also during this time that the regiment's depot was set up at the newly opened Southtown Barracks, Great Yarmouth, in 1873.

In 1874 the 2nd Battalion was sent to India again and after more fighting, firstly against the insurgent Jowaki tribes and later in the Second Afghan War, the regiment was the last in the British Army to carry its colours 'in action'. In the 1881 Cardwell Reforms of the British Army the 9th was reorganised and retitled The Norfolk Regiment. 'Rule Britannia' was adopted as the regimental march, replacing their old tune 'Young May Moon'.

In 1886–7 Britannia Barracks were built by Norwich City Council and presented to The Norfolk Regiment as its first permanent depot. In the same year the 1st Battalion went to Burma, and again in 1892, while the 2nd Battalion, quickly followed by three volunteer companies raised from the Norfolk Volunteer Battalions, went to fight in the South African War, 1899–1902.

Detachments of the regiment took part in smaller actions and expeditions such as the Relief of Peking, Somaliland and Tibet in the early years of the twentieth century. The regiment enjoyed a brief respite in the peace of India with grand parades, durbars and good living. Halcyon days were also enjoyed at home; through Haldane's Reforms the army of Queen Victoria was now modernised and reorganised, many of the proud new units taking part in fine parades to honour coronations, royal visits and grand reviews of the new territorial force. This equilibrium was shattered in August 1914 with the outbreak of the First World War.

The Norfolk Regiment furnished nineteen battalions for war service, eight of them in active service overseas. First over to France was the 1st Battalion who landed with the BEF in August 1914. The Territorials were mobilised and the 1/4th and the 1/5th served in the stinking, disease-ridden campaigns in Gallipoli, Egypt and Palestine. The 1/6th and newly raised 2/6th Cyclists served on coastal defence duties but along with all the reserve and training battalions they supplied thousands of officers and men for service at the Front throughout the war. Hundreds of men thronged to join their local regiment; local drill halls could not cope with the influx of volunteers and even uniform supplies became exhausted or piecemeal. These were the men who helped fill Lord Kitchener's appeal for 100,000 volunteers: Norfolk rapidly raised three such 'Kitchener Battalions' who were soon to be serving on the Western Front. With the widening war in the Middle East the 2nd Battalion, who had been in India when war broke out, were sent to serve in Mesopotamia, known as 'Mespot' to the troops. It was during this campaign that the 2nd Battalion led one of the last charges in the British Army where the officers were armed with drawn swords, during the Battle of Shaiba in 1915. All active service battalions of the regiment served with notable distinction. Lieutenant-Colonel John Sherwood-Kelly took command of the 9th (Service) Battalion on 20 November 1917 at Marcoing, France, and through keen personal leadership and example enabled the capture of a key position by his battalion for which he was awarded the Victoria Cross. Over 6,000 officers and men of The Norfolk Regiment died in the First World War. As a permanent memorial to these men, The Norfolk Regiment War Memorial Cottages for disabled soldiers of the regiment were established on Mousehold Heath.

In the relative peace of the interwar years the regular battalions of the regiment found themselves in the familiar round of insurgence in Ireland and the Far East, involved in actions along the north-west frontier of India and notably in Waziristan in the early 1920s.

In June 1935 in Army Order 110, on the occasion of HM King George V's birthday, Silver Jubilee and the 250th Anniversary of the raising of the regiment, the king bestowed the honour of the prefix 'Royal' in the title of the regiment.

In the late 1930s the territorial battalions enjoyed many summer camps across the county. A familiar sight was columns of soldiers in the summer months marching along roads in the coastal areas. These good and happy days are remembered with affection by prewar territorials.

The warning signs of war can be seen clearly with hindsight but in many ways the British Army was caught rather off guard when war was declared on 3 September 1939.

The 2nd Battalion, recently returned from Gibraltar, was fully mobilised at Aldershot by 10 September and crossed with the British Expeditionary Force, leaving Southampton on 20 September.

Charge at the Battle of Ferozeshalir, 22 December 1845. Under the command of Sir Hugh Gough, the 9th was accompanied by the East Surrey and West Kent regiments into battle. After the initial attack on the 21st and after resting arms on the 22nd, the troops rallied and there was no stopping them. Ferozeshalir was a victory, but at a cost, with over 2,415 British killed or wounded on the field.

Corporal McGrath, Sergeant Bayford, Corporal Neale, Lance-Corporal Harmer, Lance-Corporal Morris and Lance-Corporal Fickling of the 2nd Battalion, stand beside the spare barrel of the 100-ton gun, Rosia Bay, Gibraltar, 1908. The gun had a 14-inch calibre with a muzzle velocity of 1518 FPS (471 metres per second). Shells weighed 2,000 lbs with a 150-lb charge. It had to be crewed by thirty-five men.

They arrived in France on the 21st as the first complete infantry unit of the BEF to land, and were followed by men of the 7th Battalion (TA).

Members of the 2nd Battalion, Captain Peter Barclay and Corporal Mick Davis, were also the first men of the BEF to be decorated and in January 1940 CSM George Gristock earned the regiment's first Victoria Cross on 21 May 1940. The 2nd Battalion was part of the rearguard of the evacuating BEF; HQ Company were trapped at Le Paradis and fighting in a desperate situation. They eventually had to surrender to No. 4 Company, 2nd SS Totenkopf Regiment, and one of its senior officers, Obersturnbannführer Fritz Knochlein, saw to it that the men were marched down the lane to a meadow and summarily executed by enfilade fire from two machine-guns either end of the meadow. By a miracle two survived, eventually got home and saw the officer was brought to trial and punished for this heinous crime.

The Territorial Army was quickly mobilised in 1939 but owing to interwar decline had to be rapidly brought up to strength and trained for battle. After weathering one of the coldest winters on record guarding the Norfolk coast they were plummeted into the opening theatre of war in the Far East, fighting a new enemy – the Japanese. Along with the ill-fated 18th (Eastern) Division they were surrendered by General Percival at the fall of Singapore in February 1942. Subsequently their greatest fight was for over two years as prisoners of war in Japanese hands. Colonel A.E. 'Flicker' Knights MC, MM said: 'In spite of all the Japanese could do; the brutality of the guards, frequent beatings, humiliation and torture suffered, the men of the 4th, 5th and 6th Battalions of The Royal Norfolk Regiment never forgot they were soldiers. It was their steady discipline, inflexible courage through adversity and a native dignity and comradeship unique to Norfolk men that brought them through their horrific ordeal.'

The 2nd Battalion was raised again and sent to India and Burma in 1942 and served with distinction throughout the campaign in such epic battles as Kohima, Imphal, the crossing of the Irrawaddy and the push into Mandalay. The 2nd Battalion acquitted themselves with more individual decorations than any other battalion in the 2nd Division throughout the campaign. Their record included the Victoria Cross posthumously awarded to Captain John Neil Randle for his gallantry at Kohima on 6 May 1944. Another VC followed on 31 January 1945 when George Arthur Knowland (attached to the Commandos) singlehandedly stormed a Japanese dugout near Kangaw, Burma.

The 1st Battalion had been finishing their term in India when war broke out. On their return to England they were too late for the BEF and after much training and rumours of their services being required in one of the most important theatres of war, they were to be called for one of the most important operations of the war – Operation 'Overlord' – the Normandy landings on 6 June 1944. Rapidly followed by the 7th Battalion, both battalions had members awarded VCs early in the campaign, Corporal Sidney 'Basher' Bates at Sourdeval on 6 August 1944 and Captain David Jamieson of the 7th Battalion on 7 August 1944 at the Orne Bridgehead; Jamieson was the only Royal Norfolk soldier to live to receive his Victoria Cross.

The 7th Battalion was again decimated and the majority of its members were incorporated into the 1st Battalion a few months later. The 1st Battalion went on to distinguish itself through France, Belgium and Holland where it liberated the town of Helmond. The people have not forgotten this act and have formed the Vrienden (Friends of) the Royal Norfolk Regiment, keeping in regular contact with the veterans of that action to this day.

The 1st Battalion pressed on into Germany and on the borders engaged in the costly and horrible battle of Kervenheim, proceeding eventually to its last battle at Bremen in April 1945.

One of the greatest honours to be bestowed on the regiment came directly after the end of the war when on 3 October 1945 the Royal Norfolk Regiment was granted the Freedom of the City of Norwich, giving the regiment the privilege and distinction to march through the city with bayonets fixed, bands playing and colours flying. Yet another distinction transpired later as the number of Victoria Crosses, five in total, awarded to the regiment during the Second World War, surpassed all other regiments in the British Army.

At the conclusion of the Second World War the 1st Battalion continued serving in Germany as part of the British Army of the Rhine. Their next action was to be in the Korean War followed by service in Hong Kong and peacekeeping in Cyprus in the turbulent times of an uneasy peace. National Service had swelled the ranks of the regiment in postwar years, many of those men fighting wars in 'peace time'. Sadly their deeds and sacrifices are often forgotten or not recognised in the history books.

Reform in the British Army was to hit the Royal Norfolk Regiment hard; for the final time the 2nd Battalion was disbanded in 1948. The biggest blow came after the Defence White Paper of April 1957, announcing that the number of units in the British Army must be reduced. The first step in this reduction was the amalgamation of certain infantry regiments consequently in 1959 the Royal Norfolk Regiment ceased to exist upon its amalgamation with the Suffolk Regiment to form the 1st East Anglian Regiment. A further amalgamation of all the old East Anglian Regiments followed in 1964, creating the Royal Anglian Regiment.

For those of us who know and love the 'Holy Boys' and the grand lady, the Figure of Britannia, there will always be the Royal Norfolk Regiment, carried in our hearts with the spirit and pride forged over almost 300 years of continuous service all over the world. Over the years it has been my honour and pleasure to meet many veterans of this grand old regiment; the comradeship, unselfish pride they demonstrate, unstinting help, generosity and encouragement which every veteran (and often his family) without exception has given me, is a constant inspiration. Words cannot describe the pride I feel to be so closely associated with so many veterans' groups, from FEPOW to the Normandy Veterans' Association, but especially the 1st Battalion, Royal Norfolk Regiment D-Day Veterans' Association, who elected me their Honourary Secretary in 1995, one of the greatest honours of my life. This book is my tribute to all veterans of the 9th Foot, The Norfolk Regiment and The Royal Norfolk Regiment, especially those lying 'in the corner of some foreign field'. We must remember the words of the Kohima Memorial:

'When you go home tell of us and say,

For your tomorrows we gave our todays.'

Rule Britannia!

Neil R. Storey
Norwich, 1997

CARDWELL'S SOLDIERS

Herbert, Horace and Frederick Sowers, brothers newly enlisted into The Norfolk Regiment (titled so in 1881), at the new Depot at Britannia Barracks on Mousehold Heath, Norwich, late 1880s. They wear the then brand new pattern Valise Equipment, eventually universally known as the Slade-Wallace, introduced in 1888. All of these changes came from radical reform during this period in the British Army. Valuable lessons in the practicality of equipment carried were learnt during the Crimean War and from experiences on campaigns in Britain's growing Empire, as well as the necessity to provide a credible and improved image of the army as a career to enable its necessary expansion. Most of these issues were achieved by Edward Cardwell, Liberal Secretary of State for War 1868–74. The Cardwell Reforms are probably most notable for the 'localisation' of the military system, formally linking the old numbered regiments to counties and creating administrative districts (sixty-six in total) welding together regular army, militia and volunteers; for the first time regiments of the line were given fixed, permanent depots.

Officers of the 2nd Battalion, Shorncliffe, April 1873. Standing, left to right: Lt Maltby, Qtr Mr Sterret, Sub-Lt Currie, Lt Elmhurst, Lt Glennie, Lt Seaton, Dr Hoystead, Lt Clogstonn, Lt Bacon, Capt. Wright, Lt Shepherd, Lt Robertson, Lt Graves, Sub-Lt Bethell. Centre row: Capt. Germon, Capt. Roberts, Capt. Dunn, Capt. Kidsdale, Maj. Probart, Lt-Col Buchanan, Maj. Daunt, Capt. Burland, Capt. Huxham, Lt Mitchell, Paymaster Morrison. Front row: Lt Townshend, Lt Lovell, Sub-Lt Straghan, Sub-Lt Shuckburgh. The photograph was taken six years after the third raising of the 2nd Battalion.

Sergeants of the 2nd Battalion 9th Foot at Shorncliffe, 1873. (Note the cross flags worn above the stripes seated third and fourth from left and lying on the floor denoting the recruiting sergeants.) They would compete for willing recruits to enlist for the statutory twelve years service (six with the Colours and six on the Reserve). During this period it was still not the done thing to 'go for a soldier'; Cardwell's Reforms took some time to implement and the Army was mostly made up of 'old sweats' serving out their twenty-one years: '. . . with a commendable code of honour of their own, [they] were in many cases addicted to rough behaviour, heavy drinking and hard swearing'.

Officers and men of the West Norfolk Militia at the cavalry barracks, 1879. Some of their number are wearing their Indian Mutiny medals, recalling 10 November 1857 when they were embodied to serve in the emergency in which their parent regiment, the 54th (West Norfolk) Regiment of Foot (after the 1881 Reforms the 2nd Battalion Dorset Regiment), also served. On 15 July 1881 the West and East Norfolk Militia Battalions became respectively the 3rd and 4th Battalions of The Norfolk Regiment.

Chapel Field Volunteer Drill Hall, opened in October 1866 by HRH Edward, Prince of Wales. Originally the drill hall for the City of Norwich Rifle Volunteers in the 1880s, it became the headquarters and drill hall of the 1st Volunteer Battalion. It was sadly demolished in 1963 during the construction of the Norwich inner-link road.

Officers of 2nd Battalion, 9th Foot, Kabul, February 1880. Back row, left to right: Qtr-Mr Reeves, 2nd Lt Borton, Lt Straghan, Capt. Burton, Lt Shuckburgh (Adjutant), 2nd Lt Morton, Lt Thompson, Lt Lombe. Front row: 2nd Lt Belcher, Dr Walsh (Surgeon), Col. Daunt, Maj. Roberts, Capt. Cotton, Lt Griffin, Lt Govan, 2nd Lt Lugard.

A typical view of one of the fortified emplacements constructed by the sappers and miners in the Sherpur Basin, guarded by Indian soldiers and a detachment from the 2nd Battalion, Kabul, c. 1879. This entire campaign saw the battalion up against a cunning enemy, savage disease, diverse weather conditions and terrain, and hard marching from the Khyber Pass to Kabul and Jellalabad. It was also during this campaign that the 2/9th had its rear-guard attacked at Jadallak; they turned about to double down the hill to engage, but before this was done the colours carried by two subalterns were ordered not to accompany the battalion to the fight but to be taken into the fort at Kotal – shots coming over their heads. It was later found that following the recent War Office directive forbidding regimental colours to be carried into battle the 2nd Battalion have the distinction of carrying the last British infantry colours under fire.

Sir Henry Bates KCB, Colonel of the 1st Battalion, leads his troops on the march from Limerick in Ireland, 1881. Behind the beautiful countryside lay a troubled country. The battalion had been in Ireland since 1877, just one of many times the regiment had been engaged in peacekeeping there since its first tour in 1689. In 1881 there were more troubles than usual, with the Fenian Plots of revolution; soldiers were ambushed and the control of disturbances was an '. . . uncongenial and thankless task'.

Southtown Barracks at Great Yarmouth, 1885. This was the first official depot of the 9th Regiment in Norfolk when its depot companies moved here on 6 May 1873 to occupy the 31st Brigade depot. Maj. Probart, who later commanded the 1st Battalion, was in charge of this depot.

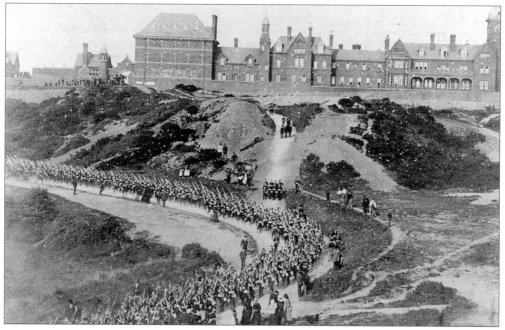

A massive column of men from Britannia Barracks march down St James's Hill, c. 1887. The depot of The Norfolk Regiment moved into its first purpose-built home in Britannia Barracks in 1887. The Barracks also acted as headquarters for the 3rd and 4th Volunteer Battalions. The site, presented to the War Office by the Mayor and Corporation of the City of Norwich, could hold 440 officers and men, including those in married quarters, and had its own hospital.

Group of past and present officers together with the Colours to the 1st Battalion, on the day of their presentation at Aldershot, 24 September 1887 by HRH The Prince of Wales. The old Colours carried since 1848 described as 'almost bare poles' were 'laid up' in Norwich Cathedral. Back row, left to right: Lt Margesson, Lt Wellesley, Capt. Loader, Lt Close, -?-, -?-. Second row: Lt Marriott, -?-, Capt. Baker, Capt. Leathes, Lt Dunn, Col. Massey, -?-, Lt Ray, -?-, Lt Inglis, Capt. Farley, -?-, -?-, -?-. Third row: Lt Peebles, Capt. Vasey, Lt Levine (holding old Queen's Colour), Lt Dods (Ensign, holding new Queen's Colour), Lt Tonge (Ensign, holding new Regimental Colour), Lt Champaign (holding old Regimental Colour), Major James, -?-, -?-. Seated: Capt. Sewell, Capt. Govan, Gen. Hanes, -?-, Gen. Buchannan, Gen. Daunt CB, -?-, Col. Stockley, Maj. Wavell, Capt. Shortt, Capt. Besher. Seated on ground: Lt Beauwick, Lt Bellamy, Lt Chater, Maj. Currie, Lt Applewaite, -?-. This was the first time that colours were presented to the regiment since the old 9th (East Norfolk) Regiment of Foot was given its full Regimental District and the title The Norfolk Regiment.

Officers and men of the 2nd Battalion Mounted Infantry Detachment at Mandalay, Burma, 1888. The detachment, consisting of 6 officers and 200 other ranks, took part in numerous operations against bandits – including one of the last operations of the expedition against the village of Tartan in May 1889. When their rifle fire could not dislodge the defenders a bayonet charge was undertaken; it proved costly and many men were killed or wounded. Lt Michel was one of the casualties. Shot in the femoral artery, he was treated under severe fire by Surgeon Capt. Le Quesne, who was later awarded the Victoria Cross for his attempt to save the life of the young Lieutenant.

Officers of 2nd Battalion, Mandalay, November 1888. Standing, left to right: Capt. Percy, Capt. Griffin, Lt Luard, Lt Trevor, Lt Close, Lt Mitchell, Lt Warburton, Lt Verner, Lt Richardson. Seated: Qtr-Mstr Grehan, Maj. Brewster, Col. Perry, Maj. Shepherd, Capt. Lombe, Capt. Borton (Adjutant). Seated on floor: Lt Brett, Lt Breakspear.

Men of the 1st Battalion, complete with band and mounted officers in the centre, 'form the square', an antiquated military manoeuvre dating back to the eighteenth century. They are pictured on the parade square at Dagshai, India, where they moved from Umballa during the hot weather season in early 1894.

Lt Knox and his winning team from the 1st Battalion at the Army of India tug-of-war competition, Umballa, 1895. In the final against the mountain batteries, the 1st's winning pull lasted for over six minutes.

Men of the 3rd (Militia) Battalion at Britannia Barracks, *c.* 1890. Col. H. Wood CB was Colonel Commanding and Alexander McCulloch (seen to the right of the photo next to the Drummer) was Barrack Sergeant. Their pay was about 1*s* per muster.

Officers and NCOs of the 1st (City of Norwich) Norfolk Rifle Volunteers, *c.* 1885. They are dressed in the scarlet tunics and glengarrys which they assumed in 1877–8 in favour of the grey frock coat and peaked cap similar to those worn by the Confederates during the American Civil War. The battalion was some 500 strong when fully mustered at their drill hall on Chapel Field. Their exercise ground was on Unthank Road and their rifle range was on Mousehold Heath.

Officers past and present gather with the Colour Party from the 2nd Battalion, then stationed at Aldershot, in front of the Officers' Mess at Britannia Barracks before the service of Laying up Colours at Norwich Cathedral, 10 August 1896. Reduced to little more than thready strips the Colours were originally presented at Corfu in 1859. On campaign longer than any man in the battalion, they had been carried in Hong Kong and India, and were the last colours carried under fire by the British Army in Afghanistan in 1879.

Col. Sir Charles Harvey Bt was born in Bracondale in 1849. Commissioned as a Sub-Lieutenant in the East Norfolk Militia in April 1874, he worked up the ranks to become Colonel of the 4th Volunteer Battalion, and retired in 1901. Always keenly interested in his old regiment, he had his own fascinating museum at his home at Rainthorpe Hall and he wrote the now rare volume *History of the 4th Battalion, Norfolk Regiment, Late East Norfolk Militia*, published in 1899. He died on 30 January 1928.

Sgt Henry Lacey, Drill and Musketry Instructor, B Company (Diss), 4th Volunteer Battalion, Norfolk Regiment, *c.* 1895. On his right forearm he wears two five-pointed stars, badges unique to other ranks and NCOs in the Volunteers and early Territorials. It denotes the wearer has qualified as 'efficient' for four years; additional stars were permitted for every further aggregate of four years. It was not unusual to see old Volunteers wearing up to eight stars.

One of the platoons of Volunteers from rural North Norfolk off to summer camp, probably on the South Denes at Great Yarmouth, *c.* 1895. Such annual camps would take place over twenty-seven days in May and June; pay would be 1*s* 6*d* a day and, often with a supplement of about a shilling out of his platoon commander's own pocket, a Volunteer would feel quite rich.

Ambulance Section of the 2nd Volunteers Battalion, Great Yarmouth, *c*. 1895. Before the formation of the Royal Army Medical Corps in 1898, far more responsibility fell to individual regiments for treatment of their casualties in the field. Here the section is seen with their Furley Litter (for transporting stretcher cases over long distances), splints and first aid kit.

Signal Section of the 1st Volunteer Battalion, *c*. 1895. Before the days of field telephones communication would have relied on sections such as these, armed with flags and proficient in semaphore. The lamps would have flashed the messages and the telescopes would have been used to observe signallers over long distances.

Men from the 2nd Battalion resting by the roadside during manoeuvres near Kinsale, Southern Ireland, *c*. 1897. On the far left is Lt-Col. L.H. Phillips mounted on his horse, while his escorts have bicycles. It is also interesting to note that there are band members behind them ready to strike up a tune as they move off.

Lt-Col. L.H. Phillips, the new commanding officer of the 2nd Battalion, with his Headquarter Company Sergeants at Fermoy, 1898. Five companies of the 2nd Battalion left Aldershot in November 1896 for Ireland; the battalion headquarters followed in January 1897 and remained there until the end of 1899, when they returned to Aldershot to prepare for their deployment to the growing conflict in South Africa.

Officers, NCOs and men of the 2nd Volunteer Service Company kitted out for service in South Africa, photographed on Mousehold Heath shortly before their departure on 16 March 1900. Two Voluntary Service Companies were rapidly raised following an appeal to the men of the four Volunteer Battalions for volunteers for active overseas service. On arrival they were attached to the 2nd Battalion.

Lt-Col. C.H. Phillips with his officers and sergeants at Bloemfontein, 1900. They had already fought in Cape Colony, at the Relief of Kimberley and with distinction at the Battle of Paardeburg. From Bloemfontein they advanced to Pretoria, a distance of 300 miles, and served in the Orange Free State, Transvaal and Johannesburg, many configurations of these actions appearing as bars on the Queen's South Africa Medal awarded to all participants.

In 1901 the reinforcements sent out to South Africa and the general state of affairs enabled Lord Kitchener to dispense with a number of volunteer companies who had come forward for service abroad. Among the twenty-three companies initially sent home was the First Norfolk Volunteer Company, which sailed from Cape Town in April 1901. This picture shows men of the 3rd Norfolks, a militia battalion embodied in January 1900, entraining for home from Norvals Point, 14 March 1902.

The men of Great Ryburgh platoon of the 3rd Volunteer Battalion after the Memorial Parade for Her late Majesty Queen Victoria, Tuesday 2 February 1901. Local volunteers joined in the parades and services all across the county. The 1st Volunteer Battalion even sent a detachment of 3 officers and 100 men under Capt. Orame for the massive parade in London.

The 2nd Battalion returned to Colchester on 10 February 1903 after the South African War. Here, pictured shortly after their arrival, the battalion's colours are returned with due ceremony by General Gatacre.

Later on 10 February every man in the 2nd Battalion was personally presented with his South African War Medal by General Gatacre. On the 16th, by invitation of the Mayor of Norwich, Lt-Col. J.R. Harvey DSO, the battalion went by train to Norwich under the command of Lt-Col. C.E. Borton CB. They marched through the city, were welcomed by a great crowd, and were given a civic reception in St Andrew's Hall.

"Bronco" Norfolk's Regimental Pet
(31 H. G. R., C.)

'Bronco', the 2nd Battalion's Regimental Pet acquired during the South African War; he had a small jacket made for him complete with medal ribbons and was even known to puff away on a pipe. A popular and amusing member of the battalion, he sadly died in Gibraltar in 1908 after drinking a pot of paint. The taxidermist executed such an awful job on their old comrade that the men of the battalion decided it would be more dignified to give 'Bronco' a full honours funeral and decent burial.

Sergeants of the 2nd Battalion at Colchester, c. 1902. They are all seen wearing their newly issued 'Broderick Caps', named after Sir John Broderick, the Secretary of State for War at the time. The caps were very unpopular and were made obsolete in 1905 except for the Royal Marine Light Infantry, who wore them throughout the First World War.

The 1st Battalion had been out in India since 1889 and the men and their families adapted well to life in the far flung Empire, which was, when not on campaign, a far more comfortable life than at home – where for many it meant tedium, unemployment and slum living conditions. This group is gathered for the camera on the occasion of Sgt Richardson's wedding to the daughter of Colour-Sgt Blake at Allahabad, India, 1895.

Presentation of India General Service Medals to 200 men of the 1st Battalion at Lebong, a small hill cantonment below Darjiling in March 1902. The medals were awarded for the men's participation between 19 October 1892 and 10 March 1903 in a small punitive expedition, under Brig.-Gen. Palmer, against the Chin Tribes.

Camp of the 2nd Battalion at Umballa, November 1902, from whence it took place in the grand manoeuvres and durbar at Delhi in celebration of the succession of King Edward VII. It was recorded that their pipe-clayed hats with '. . . yellow pugaries . . . attracted much attention'.

Children of the 2nd Battalion at the Depot Schools, Deolali, India, July 1905. It was important that education was maintained for children of servicemen whose families travelled with them. Depot schools were established in the mid-nineteenth century along with reforms to educate the many illiterate soldiers. In 1849 the Duke of Wellington ordered that all recruits must attend school daily during their initial training. Further reforms in the 1860s brought about 1st–4th Class Army Certificates of Education; from 1890 a private soldier could not draw full proficiency pay until he had gained his 3rd Class Certificate.

Lt Arthur Hadow, 1st Battalion, who in December 1903 was charged with the responsibility of a Maxim Gun Detachment from his battalion. This detachment and four companies of the Royal Fusiliers made up the mountain battery that provided the military escort for Col. Francis Younghusband's expedition to Tibet.

1st Battalion Maxim Gun Detachment in Tibet, 1904. It numbered eighteen men in total, namely Lt A.L. Hadow, Sgt F. Lake, Cpl P. Green, L-Cpl S. Galey, L-Cpl R. Taylor and Ptes J. Coleman, R. Durrant, W. Edwards, H. Green, E. Jiggins, R. Lemmon, R. Madgett, J. Moore, R. Osborne, G. Rand, C. Stannard, J. Stevens and W. Smith. Lt Hadow was mentioned in despatches and all men received the Tibet Medal with Gyantse Bar when it was authorised in February 1905 for their service between 13 December 1903 and 23 December 1904. Today these rare awards are some of the most desirable for collectors of British Army medals.

Study of a member of the Maxim Gun Detachment in Tibet, 1904 — with one of the twelve pack-mules used to carry supplies, Maxim machine-guns and ammunition. Much had to be improvised because such weaponry had never been carried over such distances and terrain before; they even invented their own drill enabling them to open fire from the line of march in forty seconds.

Men of the 1st Volunteer Battalion led by Maj L. Prior march up St Andrew's Hill, Norwich, past Charles Payne's Gas Fitter's shop on to Redwell Street, on their way to parade for the unveiling of the Norfolk South African War Memorial, 17 November 1904.

Pictured as the half-hour chimes ring out across Norwich at 2.30 p.m. on 17 November 1904, Bandmaster Ernest Elford raises his baton for the band of the 2nd Battalion to strike up the National Anthem as Maj.-Gen. A.S. Wynne CB pulls the cords releasing the Union flags to unveil the panels bearing the names of 310 officers, NCOs and men who had died serving in the various Norfolk corps during the South African War of 1899–1902. The square at the unveiling comprised 120 men from the 2nd Battalion under Capt. Cramer-Roberts and their band (having travelled down in the morning from Colchester), 3rd Battalion from the Depot, a contingent of the 1st Volunteer Battalion, a squadron of the 7th Dragoon Guards and a contingent from the Norfolk Yeomanry. The ceremony ended after speeches from General Wynne and the Mayor followed by the 2nd Battalion firing three volleys, with the band playing 'camps' between volleys, and the buglers finally sounding the Last Post.

Men of A Company Bearer Section (Long Stratton), and bandsmen of the 4th Volunteer Battalion enjoy pies and pints on the Rectory Lawn at Long Stratton after parade, August 1905.

Men of the 3rd Volunteer Battalion with their ambulance van at the Sedgeford May Day Carnival, 1906. They wear slouch hats – a distinction from the days of the Boer War, where the Volunteer Battalions served with distinction, and proudly emblazoned the South Africa Battle Honour awarded to them on their colours.

Sergeants wearing Broderick hats and canvas bandoliers from the respective cyclist sections of the Volunteer Battalions at annual training camp, *c.* 1904. The bandolier was introduced to the British Army during the South African War, and was based on those made of leather worn by Boer Commandos; it held up to 100 rounds of ammunition, avoiding the loss of rounds and allowing for more mobility. The bandolier caused the demise of the Slade Wallace Equipment of 1888. Cyclist sections in The Norfolk Regiment hove back to Col. Dawson's command of the 1st Volunteer Battalion in the 1890s. From 1900 all four Volunteer Battalions had cyclist companies, and in the Norfolk Volunteer Infantry Brigade the four companies were formed into one composite battalion at annual training camp.

Officers and men of A (King's Lynn) Company, 3rd Volunteer Battalion, 1906. Uniformed in khaki, seated third from left is the then newly commissioned Arthur Deveraux Patrick, (partner in the well-known King's Lynn Timber Merchants, Patrick & Thompson). He became Commanding Officer of B Company, 5th Battalion in February 1914 and was sadly killed in action leading his troops in Gallipoli on 12 August 1915.

SECTION TWO

HALDANE'S REFORMED ARMY

Drum Major Babbage and Boy Grant of the 1st Battalion at Warley, 1908; over the ensuing five years they were to see the implementation of some of the most influential reforms and restructuring in the history of the British Army. Richard Burdon Haldane, the new Liberal Government's War Secretary, had the duty of implementing the Esher Report. With his team of advisers (including a young Douglas Haig) he provided the army with official manuals laying down, in detail, staff responsibilities and procedures in the form of Field Service Regulations. The greatest task implemented was, however, the complete reorganisation of the Home Field Army and Reserve System, which created the Territorial Force from the old Volunteer System and the provision of the British Expeditionary Force (BEF).

Men of the newly created 5th Battalion, Territorial Force on camp at Hunstanton, *c.* 1908. Haldane's Reforms, introduced from April 1908, arranged the Territorial Force on a divisional basis like the Expeditionary Force. The East Anglian Division required only two eight-company battalions, each of 1,009 officers and men of The Norfolk Regiment. There were four battalions of Norfolk Volunteers and they had to be amalgamated into two; this was done by uniting the 1st and 4th Volunteer Battalions and the 2nd and 3rd Volunteer Battalions into the 4th and 5th (Territorial) Battalions. Also in Haldane's scheme provision was made for a 6th (Territorial) Battalion Cyclists, raised initially with 4 officers, and 176 NCOs and men from all the old Volunteer Battalions. There was a lack of conformity in uniform throughout this period of rapid and fluid change, especially in the new Territorial Force. This photograph illustrates the diversity of the time; some volunteers still have their old scarlet tunics bearing volunteer insignia, while some have a suit of khaki as initially issued to the Regular Army in 1902, with red and white cloth regimental titles worn on the shoulder below the shoulder strap and the cloth battalion number appearing below that. Some wear the new service dress with shoulder straps, while others still have the old detachable shoulder cord piped with red infantry arm-of-service colour.

A rare picture of men of the 1st Battalion in the early pattern fatigue overalls rafting during an exercise at Aldershot, *c.* 1909. From the turn of the century and the publication of the *Text Book of Field Engineering* by Colonel Phillips, formerly Professor of Fortification at the RMC, rafts and bridges played a regular role in large training exercises of the British Army. 'Rafting' was described as follows: '. . . the bridge is put together in different portions along the shore, each raft consisting of two or more piers . . . the rafts are successively rowed, towed or warped into their positions in the bridge and anchored; the roadway is then formed across the interval between them. This method has the advantage of allowing a large number of men to be simultaneously employed.'

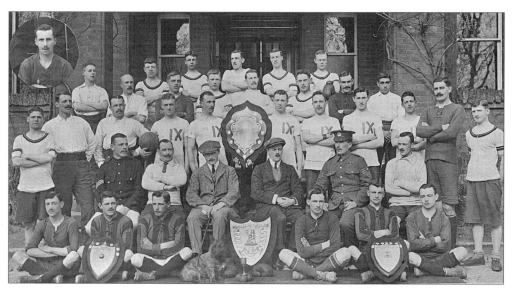

Sportsmen of A Company, 1st Battalion, Aldershot. These men were winners of the Grand Challenge Shield between 1909 and 1912, and winners of the Sports Shield, Cricket Shield and Football Shield in 1911 and 1912, and of the regimental cross-country run for six years in succession.

On his visit to Norwich on 25 October 1909, HM King Edward VII reviewed the whole territorial force of Norfolk on Mousehold Heath, where he presented the 4th, 5th and 6th Battalions of The Norfolk Regiment with Colours.

HM King Edward VII, seated centre, pauses for the camera with the officers of the 4th Battalion to record his visit to the Chapel Field drill hall on Monday 25 October 1909. Having been escorted from the grand review on Mousehold Heath, His Majesty was entertained to luncheon here by Col. Hugh Barclay VD.

Men of the 4th Battalion (late 1st Volunteer Battalion) band pose for the photographer in front of their Headquarters, the Chapel Field drill hall, after their parade for King Edward VII, 1909.

A detachment of men from 1st Battalion sent down to London from Malplaquet Barracks at Aldershot under Lt.-Col. Marriott to represent the regiment and to honour its Colonel-in-Chief, King Edward VII, at his funeral procession on 20 May 1910.

Men of G Company, 4th Battalion Territorials under Capt. W.A.C. Burrell, formed up in the Market Place at the ceremony of the Proclamation of King George V in Thetford, Tuesday 10 May 1910. After the announcement was given by the mayor, Mr Robert Tilley, the Territorials gave the Royal Salute and the band rendered the National Anthem; this was followed by three cheers for the new king and queen.

The band of the 4th Battalion proudly march down London Street on the occasion of King George V's first official visit to Norwich, 28 June 1911.

King George V removes his top hat to return the salute of lowered colours from the 4th Volunteer
Battalion on his first official visit to Norwich, 28 June 1911. He leaves St Andrew's Hall having inspected
the newly formed 6th (Cyclist) Battalion with a mounted escort of the King's Own Royal Regiment,
Norfolk Yeomanry under Col. Harvey Barclay CVO, TD, ADC.

A fine spectacle of Empire: a Guard of Honour of 100 Rank and File under Capt. F.C. Lodge is inspected by King George V at Apollo Bandar, Bombay, 2 December 1911. This was the first occasion on which an English reigning sovereign visited his Indian Empire. King George also attended his Coronation durbar at Delhi in 1912. It was the singular honour of The Norfolk Regiment to provide his first and last military Guards of Honour.

Officers of the 2nd Battalion gathered together with their commanding officer Lt-Col. A.H. Luard DSO at Belgaum, India, shortly before his hand over to Lt-Col. E.C. Peebles DSO on 1 September 1912.

Men from London serving with the 2nd Battalion, Belgaum, 1912. Often large numbers of men came from London into The Norfolk Regiment, recruited during the various battalions' stays and duties in and around the capital – notably in April 1894 when the 1st Battalion relieved the Scots Guards at the Tower of London. On 9 June the battalion lined the streets from Mark Lane station to the Royal Mint for the opening of Tower Bridge by the Prince of Wales.

What a fine show! The gymnastics team of the 2nd Battalion demonstrate part of the display they trained for and performed at the Delhi Durbar, 1912. I wonder how long they had to hold still for the camera.

The Royal Army Temperance Association gathers complete with their medals, worn on the opposite side to military decorations and awards, Belgaum, 1912. Soldiers had a long reputation for drunkenness and violence, consequently temperance, education and religious associations were heavily encouraged and even incorporated into training to combat this old stigma. Col. Luard commented on the 2nd Battalion's first twelve months in India: despite not being a 'teetotal corps' there were only four instances of drunkenness.

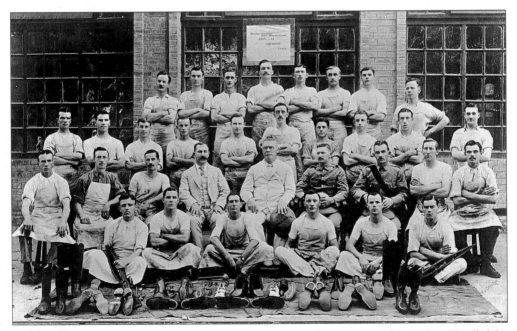

2nd Battalion men attending a shoemaking class, Cawnpore, India, *c.* 1913. Life in India still called for some self sufficiency and after a spate of thefts from local cobblers and the need for future independence in less hospitable conditions the army established shoemaking and cobbling classes for British soldiers.

2nd Battalion cooks, mess staff, wallers and bearers, known as the 'Black Watch', Belgaum, India, 1913.

The Sergeant-Major gives 'eyes right' as officers and men of B and C Companies, 1st Battalion, march, colours flying, past their Colonel-in-Chief, King George V and his mounted entourage at the King's Birthday Parade on Laffan's Plain, Aldershot, 4 June 1912.

Men of F Company, 5th Battalion, leaving for Territorial Camp on Mousehold Heath from Sheringham station, July 1910. Standing, left to right: Jack Palmer, Fred Abbs, Sidney Rolfe, Harry Barney, Teddy Moore, Billy Lusher, John Grice. On one knee in front: Jack Battrick.

Kit bags loaded on to army carts ready to take them to the Battalion Camp on Stuston Common near Diss, *c.* 1910. Beside the rear cart is Lt S. Coxon in his greatcoat; fallen in behind him are his men of D Company, 4th Battalion from their headquarters on Denmark Street in Diss. They are kept in step by Colour-Sgt Thomas Stubbs, their drill instructor, standing in front of them.

'Happy as the Day that the Sergeant gets his Pay.' Pay Parade Group of A Company, 5th Battalion encamped at the first combined manoeuvres of the three Norfolk Territorial Battalions at Sheringham, July 1910.

Hot work here as men of the 4th Battalion break into shirt sleeve order while trenching at Thetford Camp, August 1911, when the East Anglian Territorial Division was encamped together for the first time under Maj.-Gen. the Hon. J.H. Byng. It is sobering to think that many of the men pictured here would need to occupy such dug-outs for real only three years after this picture was taken.

Tent Orderlies waiting with their billy-cans for issue of tea outside the Quarter-Master's stores at Thetford Camp, 1911. Breakfast, before the dining or mess hall system for other ranks, would usually consist of tea, a bread ration and an ounce of butter for each man – collected by Tent Orderlies, taken back for themselves and nine of their comrades, and eaten at their tent.

The splendid turnout of military bands has always been a popular attraction at county and local shows. Here we see the band of the 5th Battalion at the Royal Show, Trowse, Norwich, June 1911.

A magnificent full turnout of the 4th Battalion, including the Maxim Gun Detachment, band and mounted officers for one of their 'Field Days' – a chance for wives, girlfriends, family and friends to see what their 'Saturday Night Soldier' got up to at weekends. This was held on the South Denes at Great Yarmouth, September 1911.

The local priest gives the Sunday sermon from an altar of drums at the Great Yarmouth 'Field Day' and Camp of the 4th Battalion, 1911.

Men of A and HQ Companies, 6th (Cyclist) Battalion ready for inspection at Boughton Park Camp, Kettering, Northamptonshire, September 1913.

A roadside halt while on manoeuvres for men of the 6th (Cyclist) Battalion, Kettering, September 1913.

This fine turn-out is the Guard of Honour provided by men of the 2nd Battalion for Lord Willingdon on his visit to their station at Belgaum, India, 19 November 1913.

The Christmas trimmings give the 2nd Battalion's Sergeants' Mess at Belgaum a festive feel for their seasonal celebrations in 1913, although the temperature was over 100 degrees outside. The 2nd Battalion remained stationed in Belgaum until 3 November 1914, when it embarked for the Persian Gulf to play its role in the First World War.

Colour Party of the 4th Battalion ready for parade at Holkham Park Camp, July 1914.

Men gather in their companies to hear the Field Service given from behind an altar of drums at Holkham Park Camp, 1914.

Men of the Norfolk and Suffolk Territorial Brigade (about 2,000 strong) under Col. R. Bayard DSO march past the Earl of Leicester, Lord Lieutenant of Norfolk, on Holkham Park Camp, July 1914. This was the last camp of the Territorials before the First World War; men had hardly returned to their homes when the mobilization order of 29 July 1914 was issued.

On 20 November 1912 the 1st Battalion was sent to Palace Barracks, Holywood, near Belfast, Northern Ireland. Taking a strong selection of sporting teams, they were winners of the Irish Army Cup 1912–13. Back row, left to right: Cpl W. Bartram, Pte D. Nicholls, L-Sgt P. Witherick, Cpl A. Hurrell (Team Captain), Pte F. Barrett, L-Cpl F. Taylor, Sgt Preston. Front row: Pte G. Calver, Cpl A. Bishop, L-Cpl A. Loombe, Band Master George Dean (Hon. Sec.) Lt A.E.V. Briard, L-Cpl R. Bishop, Pte A. Smith, Pte H. Atkins, Pte G. Daniels.

D Company, 1st Battalion rugby team, winners of the Regimental Rugby Trophy, Holywood, 1914. Back row, left to right: L-Cpl Augarde, Pte Betts, L-Cpl Johnson, L-Cpl Wilkins, Cpl Watts, L-Cpl Lewis, Cpl Newstead, Pte Wilkins. Seated: CSM Galey, Lt E.F.V. Briard, Capt. E.N. Snepp, Capt. R. Clarke, Capt. E.H.T. Broadwood, Lt J.B. Oakes. Seated on ground: Pte Steward, Pte Leader, Pte Ives, L-Cpl Gout.

THE GREAT WAR

The faces of war. Men of a Norfolk Regiment Service or 'Kitchener' Battalion leaving for war service, Thorpe Station, Norwich, September 1914. The idyllic images of a gentleman's war over by Christmas, believed by so many of these young men, were soon shattered by the bloodshed, mud, infestation and sheer hell that was trench warfare.

Officers of the 1st Battalion at Belfast, shortly before leaving for France, 1914. Back row, left to right: 2nd Lt Patteson, 2nd Lt Willis, Lt O'Connor, Lt Jephson. Third row: Lt Foley, Lt Reeve, Lt Broadwood, Capt. Bowlby, Lt Lightfoot, Lt Paget. Second row: Capt. Megaw, Capt. Clark, Lt Smith, Lt Holland, Lt Briard, Lt Nixon, 2nd-Lt Boosey, 2nd-Lt Oakes, Lt Openshaw. Front row: Capt. Brundell-Bruce, Capt. Snepp, Maj. Orr DSO, Lt-Col Ballard, Capt. Cressell (Adjt), Maj. Done, Capt. Luard DSO. Six of these officers were wounded and ten killed during the First World War, seven of them before the end of 1914.

Some of the men of the 1st Battalion in front of one of their barrack blocks at Palace Barracks, Holywood, Belfast, 1914. Mobilization for France was completed by 10 August and the battalion left for Le Havre on the 14th, proceeding to Le Cateau by train where the British Expeditionary Force (BEF) was assembling. These were the men of 1914: they fought at Mons, Le Cateau, The Marne, Aisne, La Basee and the 1st Ypres, proof enough that this war was not going to be over by Christmas.

Pte Bertie Turner newly kitted out in his uniform and 1908 Pattern Webbing, standing in front of Britannia Barracks, early 1915. Introduced after the ineffective performance of the 1903 equipment for infantrymen and not wishing to return to the impracticalities of the Slade-Wallace Equipment, the 1908 Pattern Webbing was a redesigned equipment carrying woven-cotton webbing, devised by Maj. Burrowes of the Royal Irish Fusiliers and the Mills Web Equipment Company. Note that the left-hand pouches have the 1914 modification, retainer straps, introduced because the old fitting caused the pouch to snag open and drop ammunition when the soldier leaned against the trench parapet in the firing position. This pattern of equipment was popularly adopted by the British and Commonwealth armies until 1937.

L-Cpl (Later Sgt) Albert Armes, 9th Battalion (sadly he died of wounds on 4 March 1917) pictured in 1914, wearing the Pattern 1914 Leather Infantry Equipment. The outbreak of war in 1914 found the Mills Equipment Company unable to meet the demand for hundreds of thousands of sets of the 1908 Pattern Webbing Equipment needed to equip Kitchener's Army. Orders for a million sets of leather equipment consisting of good quality, stoutly sewn brown leather with brass rivets and buckles to ensure maximum strength were placed with manufacturers in Britain and America. Although it was only originally designed as a stop gap for training purposes, it was not long before troops were using it in all theatres of war.

The order for full mobilization of the Territorial Army reached both the 4th and 5th Battalions on the evening of 4 August 1914, a few hours before the formal declaration of war. The following day men from all platoons mustered into their companies at their local town headquarters, then proceeded to their battalion headquarters – the 1/4th at Norwich and the 1/5th at East Dereham. This picture shows the Aylsham Detachment of C Company, 5th Battalion who paraded in the Market Place, after being addressed by their commanding officer, Major Thomas Purdy, in the Town Hall; prayers were offered by the vicar. From there they marched headed by their band to the Great Eastern railway station, where they were pictured ready to entrain for their depot at East Dereham.

The companies of the 5th Battalion mustering, kit bags in hand on East Dereham Market Place during the afternoon of 5 August 1914. Each man was taken on arrival to the local Assembly Rooms, where he was examined for contagious diseases. By nightfall over 800 men were resting in comandeered accommodation in the town.

Men of the 4th Battalion, its companies from Norwich and District, assembled at the drill hall in Chapel Field, Norwich, on the morning of 5 August 1914. They are pictured as they arrive at their comandeered billets at the City of Norwich Schools on Newmarket Road; men rest with their large packs still on as the sergeants check their muster rolls.

Men of A Company, 3rd (Special Reserve) Battalion in front of St Michael at Coslany Church shortly after their mobilization on Saturday 8 August 1914. Originally one of the old militia units, the battalion contained initially all ex-servicemen or mostly 'old and bold'. They recruited and trained thousands of men, who made up 242 drafts to the various Expeditionary Forces.

Lt-Col. Bernard Henry Leathes Prior surveys the coastline at Cromer in 1914. He was awarded the duty of raising the cyclist battalion alloted to The Norfolk Regiment after the Haldane Reforms. A successful and popular battalion, the 6th grew rapidly under this charismatic leader. Previously having served in the South African War, Lt-Col. Prior went on to command the 9th Battalion from 1916 to 1918. He was awarded the DSO and Bar for his distinguished service.

When war broke out in 1914, members of the 6th Cyclists were mobilised to war stations under the Home Defence Scheme between Wells and Gorleston on coastal defence duties coordinated from their headquarters at North Walsham. Pictured is a member of the 1/6th at Cromer in 'riding order' in 1914. He wears the Imperial Service badge above his right breast, denoting him a volunteer for overseas service, registered before 30 September 1914.

Some of the Norfolk men who responded to the formidable 'Your Country Needs YOU' poster showing Lord Kitchener and his imposing pointing finger, parading on Carrow Fields, Norwich, August 1914.

'Kitchener Men', as they became known, immediately entered a strict regime of physical training, drill and discipline. Pictured on Chapel Field Gardens in early October 1914, men exercise before breakfast.

On the march down Newmarket Road it can be noted that 'Kitchener Men', owing to the sudden influx of such volunteers, were poorly equipped and uniformed; men in more or less complete uniforms are in the front ranks but further back uniforms become piecemeal. Men were gradually kitted out as supplies arrived with the Quartermaster – a jacket for one man, trousers and puttees for another, and so on.

Some of the men of the 8th Service Battalion, 1914, wearing 'Kitchener Blue' uniform. Owing to the massive number of volunteers, khaki uniforms and webbing equipment supplies began to run out. Consequently, the stop gap was filled with the blue smocks and Victorian Slade-Wallace equipment pictured. Later the uniform was sent for the use of prisoners of war, and after the war was issued to inmates in criminal lunatic asylums.

Eventually all the 'Kitchener Men' were fully uniformed. This finely turned out detachment on Chapel Field Gardens in 1914 is ready to join comrades from the three 'Kitchener Battalions' of Norfolk men training at St Martin's Plain, Shorncliffe.

Men of the Norfolk service battalions on the march on St Martin's Plain, Shorncliffe, 1914. At last fully armed with Long Lee-Enfield rifles and the majority of webbing issued, they were able to train on their 15-rounds-a-minute practice on the ranges. There were still chronic shortages: cutlery had to be shared, fifteen men shared each bell tent and the food was based around hard issue biscuits, 'stiff' bread and bully beef. This was all capped off with much of the drill instruction coming from pre-war, mobilised reserve NCOs, conversant only with the drill evolutions of 1870 and the 'ever popular' innoculations against typhoid, leaving recipients with throbbing arms and heads.

New recruits for the 4th (Territorial) Battalion march down Earlham Road, 1914. It was said that every time they marched out a few more men would join on the parade and volunteer. From south and east Norfolk and Norwich upwards of 700 men were recruited in the first four weeks from the outbreak of war. Many ex-servicemen or National Reservists enlisted into the 4th Battalion, so many that a 2/4th was created to administer their numbers. Barracking the men in military buildings in the city was impossible, so men were billeted with subsistence in private houses. By December 1914 well over 1,000 men had enlisted into the 5th Battalion. With about 450 men already at the depot the 2/5th was a very necessary creation. Six officers from the 1/5th, stationed at Colchester, were despatched back to East Dereham to organise two provisional companies and to begin training in earnest. The majority of the troops were billeted with local residents at the rate of 2s 6d a day.

Distributing hats and badges, the final part of uniform, to the new recruits of the 2/5th Battalion on Quebec Street, East Dereham, September 1915.

Cooks of the 5th Battalion – busy men who had to cater for over 1,000 men every day – in front of the 5th Battalion Headquarters on Quebec Street, East Dereham, September 1914.

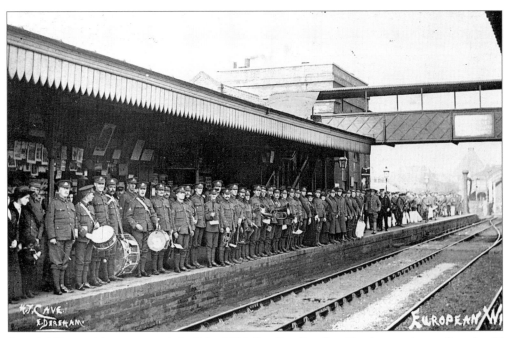

Over 1,000 men (eleven companies) of the 2/5th Battalion line East Dereham station on Saturday 12 December 1914, having marched through the town preceded by their band, before travelling to Peterborough.

Men of the 2/5th Battalion gather in front of Peterborough station, 12 December 1914. Their greatcoats are rolled up and worn across their bodies. The regimental policeman (far right, wearing the Military Police band on his cuff) keeps a watchful eye over the proceedings.

The 2/5th Battalion march through Peterborough to their billets, 12 December 1914. Early in January 1915 the 2/5th organised a recruiting march through Norfolk, visiting the principal county towns. The battalion band and a hand-picked company of men obtained a great number of fine recruits who, joining the battalion at Peterborough, brought it up to strength.

Guard Room personnel and sentries (in greatcoats, webbing and rifles with fixed bayonets) of the 1/6th Cyclists, Great Yarmouth, in early 1915. Stationed throughout the freezing cold winter on coastal duties, their lives consisited of constant mounted patrols around the town and marsh area – they became known as the 'Gas Pipe Cavalry'. The battalion's first shots in anger were fired on the night of 19 January 1915 when Norfolk was raided and bombed by Zeppelins. The cyclists, firing consistant volleys, inflicted minor damage on the low-flying Zep.

Men of the 3rd (Reserve) Battalion at the drill hall, York Road, Great Yarmouth, holding an almost intact Zeppelin bomb recovered from Crown Road. This was one of several dropped on the town on 19 January 1915, causing two fatalities and numerous casualties from flying glass, shrapnel and collapsed buildings.

Men of The Norfolk Regiment assist in the clearance of wreckage in King's Lynn after the raid of 19 January 1915. Two Zeppelins had made landfall over the north Norfolk coast; one turned and skirted the coast, bombing Great Yarmouth; the other dropped the first bomb on Sheringham and followed inland, dropping a further bomb on Snettisham and finally on King's Lynn where two fatalities were inflicted.

Captain W.G. Jacomb-Hood, seated front row centre, with the men of his company of 1/6th Cyclists on the beach at West Runton in 1915. Shortly after this photograph was taken, the 1/6th were relieved from coastal defence duties by the Royal Naval Air Service Mobile Anti-Aircraft Brigade and most of the men were sent to the 8th (Service) Battalion in France, serving on the Somme. A holding company of the battalion and riding school at Worstead remained on defence duties until 1918 when they were sent on a stinking cattle boat on peacekeeping duties in Ireland. They were stationed in Tralee, Castle Mayo and Randalstown until 1919 when they returned to Norwich and were disbanded.

A 'Half-Crown Holy Boy', a member of the 2/6th Cyclist Battalion pictured shortly after its raising at Bridlington in October 1914. His kit demonstrates the desperate need for new equipment for the growing army during this period. He wears the most basic and out of date webbing, and an 1888 Slade-Wallace belt and pouches. Even cap badges were in short supply and men like this volunteer were issued with collar badges to wear in their headgear. Armed with a charger loading Lee-Enfield rifle Mk 1 he stands by his only piece of new kit, his Mk 4 2nd Type army issue bicycle.

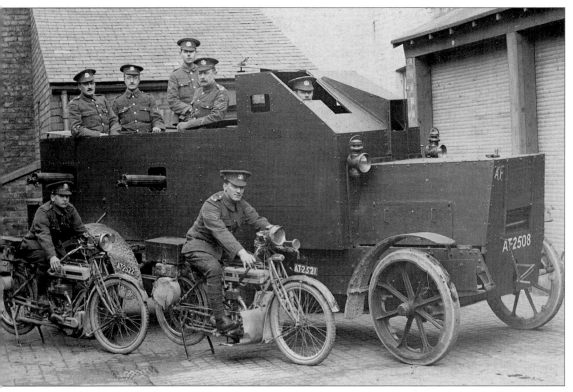

As the 2/6th grew and received better equipment, they were even issued with one of the latest War Office trial armoured cars, here pictured with the men of the Motor Section of the 2/6th at Bridlington in August 1915. This particular type of armoured car, based on a B-Type bus chassis, was condemned by an Admiralty expert for its thin armour. Its type was not adopted by the British Army and the few extant experimental models never left the country.

Officers of the 1/4th Battalion at Bury St Edmunds, 1915. Barracked in the town with men of the 1/5th, they all had a narrow escape when Zeppelins dropped over fifty bombs in one raid on the town on 30 April. Back row, left to right: Lts Corke, T.N. Flatt, W.W. Flatt, 2/Lt King, Lts Morgan, Hampton, 2/Lt Culley, Lts Boswell, Taylor, 2/Lts Steel, Collison, Caton, Jewson, Lt and Qmr Moore. Centre row: Capts Fisher, Jewson, Page, Burrell, Maj Fletcher, Col J.R. Harvey DSO, Maj Hines, Capt and Adjt E.H. Montgomerie, Capts Rudd, Back, Hughes. Front row: 2/Lts Bradshaw, Thurgar, Burrell, Spackman, Elliott, de Poix, White, 2/Lt Sir T.R. Berney Bt, 2/Lt G.H. Wood.

Men of B Company, 4th Battalion shortly before leaving from Liverpool on 29 July 1915 aboard the SS *Aquitania*, along with the 1/5th Battalion as part of the 54th Infantry Division. Brigaded with the 1/5th Suffolks and 1/8th Hampshire, they constituted the 163rd Infantry Brigade bound for Gallipoli and the Dardanelles.

Officers of the 1/5th Battalion, Watford, 1915. Back row, left to right: Lt T. Oliphant, Lt V.M. Cubitt, Lt G.W. Birkbeck, 2nd Lt M.B.G. Proctor-Beauchamp, 2nd Lt A.E.A. Culme-Seymour, Capt. A.H. Mason, Lt A.E.A. Beck, Capt. E. Gay, Capt. A.C.M. Coxon, Capt. E.R. Woodwark, 2nd Lt M.F. Oliphant, Capt. F.R. Beck. Middle row: Capt. E.R. Cubitt, Capt. A.D. Patrick, Maj. W.J. Barton, Lt-Col. H.G. Proctor-Beauchamp, Capt. A.E.M. Ward (Adjutant), Capt. A. Knight. Front row: 2nd Lt W.G.S. Fawkes, 2nd Lt W. James, 2nd Lt S.C. Larn, 2nd Lt M.B. Buxton, Lt A.R. Pelly.

Men of A Company (King's Company, Sandringham), 5th Battalion while on manoeuvres at Watford, July 1915. Many of these men and the officers pictured above fell in just one action in the Gallipoli Peninsula on 12 August 1915. Sir Ian Hamilton's despatch stated: '. . . the Colonel, with 16 Officers and 250 men, still kept pushing on, driving the enemy before them. . . . Nothing more was ever seen or heard of them. They charged into the forest, and were lost to sight or sound. Not one of them ever came back.' These statements have led to a great deal of conjecture over the years, but serious research shows that some men did survive – although it is thought the majority of those mentioned did push too far and ended up being captured and executed shortly after.

The first parade of the Norwich Volunteer Training Corps on 15 December 1914. Raised after an advertisement in the *Eastern Daily Press* and a grand meeting in the Assembly Rooms, 276 names were given with a view to starting a local VTC unit for home defence in the event of an enemy infiltration or invasion.

The 1st (City of Norwich) Battalion, Norfolk Volunteers, being inspected by Colonel, the Earl of Leicester GCVO, CMG, ADC, Regimental Commandant, accompanied by Lt-Col. Leathes-Prior VD, on 26 September 1915. Rapidly uniformed in khaki fatigues, armed and trained by Col.-Sgt B.T. Bokenham, a regular from The Norfolk Regiment, the unit grew to comprise six companies, including cyclist, transport and ambulance sections.

Spurred on by the patriotic verve of the county, further units were raised under the banner of the Norfolk Volunteers. Here are some of the members of the volunteers at Pulham; their duty was to help haul airships into the hangars at the air station. They show the various badges worn by the volunteers; in the centre, no badge as in the early days (although the Great Yarmouth VTC did have an enamel lapel badge), on the left the lion and unicorn of the General Service, worn by miscellaneous or non-alloted units, and on the far right, the castle and scroll which bore the title of 'The City of Norwich Volunteers' or 'The Norfolk Volunteers' – eventually adopted universally by all local volunteers. Some badges exist with official pin backs. These were presented as a token of thanks to ladies who assisted in the raising of funds for the volunteers, a job actively led in Norwich by Mrs Pillow.

Men of the 8th Battalion rest by the roadside as their supply train passes during manoeuvres at Hollesley, 1915. Following the raising of the Service Battalions in Norfolk and their arrival of Shorncliffe, they entered into harsh and cold training and conditions, weathering the first winter of the war in freezing cold tents shared with fifteen of their comrades, seas of mud and abysmal equipment; even cutlery had to be shared. Men were far happier when the better weather of late spring 1915 came.

Mules of the supply train of the 8th Battalion during manoeuvres with the 6th Royal Berkshire Regiment at Hollesley, 1915. Along with the 10th Essex and 8th Suffolk Regiment these battalions made up the 53rd Brigade of the 18th Divisions which embarked for France, with their mules, on 25 July 1915.

Men of the 2/4th Battalion on the march led by Col. Edward Mornement CBE, TD, who commanded the battalion which was raised in September 1914 at the Chapel Field drill hall in Norwich, seen here training near Lowestoft, summer 1915. Men of the battalion were divided into 'A' General Service Category and 'B' Home Service or lower medical category; men of category 'A' joined their comrades in the Active Service overseas battalions during the winter of 1915–16.

Orchestra of the 3rd (Special Reserve) Battalion, having moved to Felixstowe (Harwich Garrison) in August 1914, is pictured at Walton-on-the-Naze in 1916 while under the command of Col. Sir Kenneth Kemp Bt, pictured seated fourth from right. Training and despatching hundreds of drafts for overseas service, at times the battalion numbered over 100 officers and 3,000 other ranks. The orchestra was a popular respite for troops and locals alike.

Men of the 9th Service Battalion at 'Battle School', Montcavrel, France, 1915. Following the intense square bashing, skill at arms and fitness instruction in England, the Service Battalions' training was completed when they arrived in France and attended a few weeks 'Battle School' with instruction in digging, wiring and warfare in the trenches, although it must be noted that some troops only spent a few days there if reinforcements were needed on the front lines. Nothing could have really prepared those men for the horrors they were going to see or experience.

Men of the 8th Service Battalion 'somewhere in France', *c.* 1916. Many wear the 'Gor Blimey' cap made of soft khaki material with flaps, which could be lowered to create in effect a Balaclava. Many still wear their emergency issue leather webbing and slung over all their shoulders are the gas mask bags. This was the only Norfolk Battalion involved on the first day of the Battle of the Somme, 1 July 1916; they made a 'good advance' that day but, as it was for the rest of the British Army, it was horrifically costly: 4 officers killed, 9 wounded, 102 other ranks killed, 219 wounded and 13 missing. By the end of that one fateful day the British Army was counting the highest number of casualties sustained on one day in its history; over 21,000 soldiers dead, thousands wounded – the flower of English manhood slaughtered on the fields of France.

Lt Kenneth Cameron Kirby, son of Hector and Jessie Kirby of Mile End Road, Norwich. He began the war in the 1/6th (Cyclist) Battalion on coastal defence duties. Assigned to the 2/4th Battalion, he was finally attached to the 7th Battalion and served in France, where he was killed on the final advance near Epehy on 18 September 1918, less than two months before the end of the war. He was twenty-two years of age, truly laid to rest in 'some corner of a foreign field' in Epehy Wood Cemetery, 18 km north-east of Peronne.

L-Cpl Ernest Burton, 8th (Service) Battalion, son of George and Eliza Burton of Bushey Common, Gressenhall near East Dereham. Like so many country lads he answered the call for King and Country. Severely wounded at the front, he was removed from the battle lines and taken across country by amublance train to the British Army Hospital at Boulogne, where he died of those wounds on 30 October 1917. He was twenty-one years of age. The tiny communities such young men came from were devastated by the losses incurred during the war; nothing was ever quite the same again.

A few moments peace in war. Colour-Sgt Gilliland and Sgt Howard of the 7th Battalion have a shave and a clean up after coming out of the trenches, Beaumont-Hamel, November 1916. Life in the trenches meant almost constantly having your feet wet or immersed in water, rations being often in short supply and at best shared, having drinking water that tasted of the petrol cans it was brought up in, rats crawling everywhere and men rapidly becoming infested with lice. Any respite to get yourself cleaned up and a little better fed away from the front line must have been a godsend.

Cpl A. Chapman being decorated with his Distinguished Conduct Medal 'in the field', France, early 1916. His comrades paraded behind. Cpl Chapman gained the award for conspicuous gallantry during several operations when he led patrols often under heavy fire, demonstrating 'remarkable intelligence and courage under fire'.

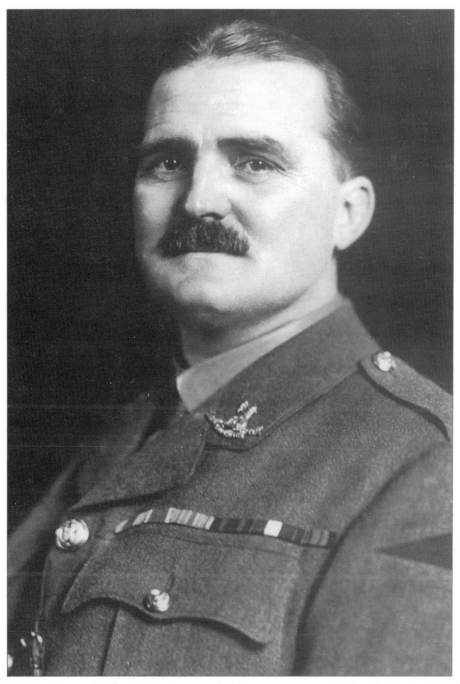

Lt.-Col. John Sherwood-Kelly VC. Having recently taken over command of the 9th (Service) Battalion, on 20 November 1917 at Marcoing, France, he saw a party of his men held up under fire. He ordered covering fire and personally led his leading company to reconnoitre the high ground held by the enemy. He took a Lewis gun team and, forcing his way through many obstacles, covered the advance of his battalion, enabling them to capture the position. Later he led a charge against some pits where five machine-guns were captured along with forty-six prisoners. He was awarded the only Victoria Cross to The Norfolk Regiment in the First World War.

The 'Dead Eye Fishing Club', one of the last glimpses of the 'good old days' in Belgaum, 1914. The 2nd Battalion had been in Belgaum, India since 1911; however, no doubt the men's thoughts turned to wondering how soon they would be sent home from their far distant station to serve in the growing war in France in August and September 1914.

Sergeants of the 2nd Battalion gather casually together, probably for the last time, Bombay, 1914. The 2nd Battalion's role in the war became uncertain when troubles flared up in the Baghdad/Basra area of Mesopotamia (known to all Tommies as Mess Pot). The 2nd Battalion comprising 23 officers, 5 Warrant Officers and 907 other ranks left Bombay on 3 November 1914 for Saniya, disembarking on the 15th, and formed part of the 18th (Indian) Brigade.

One of the most distinguished actions of The Norfolk Regiment during the First World War was on 14 April 1915 when at Shaiba the 2nd Battalion was ordered to take the Turkish trenches 'at all costs'. Realizing the desperation of the situation Lt-Col. Edward Peebles drew his sword (one of the last occasions when British officers carried swords in action), cried 'Come on the 9th', and led the fixed bayonet charge. The men, yelling all the way, kept steady as the bullets zipped around them. The Norfolk's charge sent the Turks into disarray and the trenches were captured. Tragically the victory was costly and by the late evening the battalion could hardly muster 300 men. The victory was not forgotten; for many years after the regiment annually marked Shaiba Day, and the battle honour was awarded, borne on the King's Colour.

Following the decimation of the 2nd Battalion at Ctesiphon and during the desperate siege at Kut, drafts and recovered wounded from the 2nd Norfolks and 2nd Dorset Regiment made a combined battalion known as the 'Norsets', pictured at El Orah, 1916.

The 1/4th and 1/5th Battalions, following the horrific campaign in the Dardanelles, left Mudros in November 1915 for Egypt. Comprising mostly reinforcements, very few of their number could say they were 'originals' who had left England with the first draft in July. Photographed in February 1916 are men of both battalions 'on Jankers' at Mena Camp near Cairo. Based here for six weeks, the men of the 54th Division trained drafts from England and reorganised for the defence of Suez.

Men of 4th (D) Company, 12th (Yeomanry) Battalion under Capt. J. Dawson Paul, 1917. Wearing their distinctive black and yellow pugaree patches, these men went to Gallipoli as the King's Own Royal Regiment, Norfolk Yeomanry in September 1915. Sent to Egypt in early 1916, they became the 12th Norfolks on 11 February 1917. They fought across Palestine to Jerusalem until April 1918, when they were sent as reinforcements to the Western Front.

Troops of the 2nd Battalion (37th Infantry Brigade, 14th Division) sentry posted, rifle and Lewis guns in position, guard an outpost on the Jebel Hamarin, 1918.

Officers of the 2nd Battalion taking time to read and write letters home, smoke or have a drink out of battered enamel mugs in their mess at Ruz, Mesopotamia, 1918.

Men of the 2nd Battalion blindfolding a Turkish prisoner before conducting him through British lines, Jebel Hamarin, 1918.

Men of the 1/4th as part of the 163rd Brigade, 54th Division resting by the roadside on their march to Beirut, 1918, after the battle for Gaza and the advance into Palestine and the storming of Jerusalem. From Beirut it was on into Cairo, and eventually home during 1919.

Capt. E.J. Mann gives the salute as A Company, 1st Battalion march past Lt-Gen. E.P. Strickland KCB, KBE, CMG, DSO, Colonel of the Regiment, receiving the salute, on their return from Divine Service near Nieppe Forest, June 1918.

Some of the officers and men of the 7th Battalion gather at Somain, France, January 1919. Note that many of them wear the brass bar or 'wound stripe' on the lower left arm, their frequency a testimony to the horrific fighting they had to endure. They were the first Norfolk 'Kitchener Battalion' to land in France; they fought through the Somme region, Arras, Cambrai, the Ancre and the final advance where (near the Queant–Drocourt line) the Armistice was received. Like so many other men in the regiment, it would be 1919 before they came home.

Men of the B1 Hut 2 Section 3/4th and 3/5th (Territorial Force) Combined Battalion (East Anglian Reserve Brigade) at Crowborough Camp, 1918. Raised separately in early 1915 to accommodate the huge numbers of volunteers, both battalions had their first camp at Windsor Great Park in August of that year. The two battalions, amalgamated in 1916, trained men to join active service battalions. Those pictured are members of one of the last batches to reach the fronts before the war ended.

Stationed at Shahraban at the end of hostilities, commanded by Lt-Col. F. Higson OBE, the 2nd Battalion began to send men home in January 1919 as their turn for demob came. Towards the end of February a cadre consisting of the CO, six officers and sixty-seven other ranks left 'Mess Pot' for England. Reaching Norwich on 11 April it was given the formal ceremony of welcome home the following day in the packed Market Place, where Sir George Chamberlin DL, Lord Mayor of Norwich, greeted the men.

Men of the depot hoisting the flag in Norwich Market Place, part of the ceremonial occasion during the city's Peace Day, Saturday 19 July 1919. Following a Thanksgiving and Memorial Service in the Cathedral, a massive parade of all wartime services, military and civil, marched to the city centre: prominent were the fifty men representing all battalions of The Norfolk Regiment with colours flying, led by Major Hadow.

Men from the depot pull the bier to the Rosary Cemetery, Norwich, at the funeral of 15653 Sgt Alfred Edward Hubbard, 7th Battalion. He was wounded at Hulluch, France, October 1915 and was returned home where he died on 19 December 1919 aged thirty. He was just one of hundreds of men of the regiment who do not appear in the official casualty roll of the First World War. They must not be forgotten as they all died of injuries received in that conflict.

Buglers from various battalions represent the regiment sounding the Last Post over the grave of Nurse Edith Cavell, Life's Green, Norwich Cathedral, 1919. This Norfolk heroine was shot in October 1915 charged with 'conducting soldiers to the enemy'. She had assisted wounded troops, many of them Norfolk men, to return home. This service, held on the Sunday nearest to 12 October, the anniversary of her shooting, was marked by the regiment until it amalgamated. The buglers pictured are, left to right: L-Cpl Nash, Sgt Grant, Dmr Banks, Dmr Chiverall, Sgt Grant, Dmr Buxton, Dmr Holmes and L-Cpl Howell.

THE INTER-WAR YEARS

Men of a rifle company from the 2nd Battalion in shirt sleeve order on manoeuvres, Oxney Farm Camp, when the battalion was stationed at Aldershot in 1936. In the unsure world after the First World War, the British Army, although increasingly armoured and motorised, stagnated in many ways. Its structure, uniform and equipment was really addressed too late in the 1930s, when the winds of war blew again.

A and B Company, 1st Battalion Cook House staff, Colchester, 1923. On their return to the depot from France in 1919 the 1st Battalion was rapidly sent back to its pre-war station of Ireland, and in at the deep end with the Sinn Fein rebellion. After three years of the troubles they were sent to Hyderabad Barracks, Colchester, for a short respite and recuperation of numbers from the depot.

It was not long before the 1st Battalion was called for a tour of duty in the West Indies. This postcard was produced a few days before their departure aboard the SS *Braemar Castle* on 6 September 1923, just enough time to scribble a few lines to loved ones to let them know you were off.

Band of the 1st Battalion, Prospect Barracks, near Hamilton, Bermuda, 1923. Along with C and D Companies they relieved two companies of the East Lancashire Regiment, while A and B Companies with battalion headquarters went to Jamaica to relieve the rest of the East Lancs; and thus the 1st Battalion was divided by a distance of some 1,200 miles.

Drums and Colours of the 1st Battalion guarded by the Morris brothers and accompanied by RSM Gamble in front of the Orderly Room, Moascar, Egypt, 16 January 1926. The occasion was to mark the anniversary of the Battle of Corunna. Work had ceased at 11.30 a.m. and at 12 noon the battalion complete with band paraded and marched in slow time through the barracks, halted outside the Orderly Room where the drums were piled, colours crossed above and double sentries posted to enable the men to inspect them until 2 p.m. – when they were escorted back to the Officers' Mess.

Capt J.B. Oakes seated centre of A (Machine-Gun Company), which he commanded, 2nd Battalion, Aldershot, 1927. Following experiments with Lewis Guns in 1926, the 2nd Battalion was reorganised on an experimental formation of HQ Wing, three service companies and one machine-gun company for manoeuvres of 1927. The system was adopted until the mid-1930s.

Signal Section of the 1st Battalion, Abassia, Egypt, 1928. The section was under the command of Lt Pope and 2nd Lt Carroll, seated centre of the front row. At the time all ranks in the section were swotting for their annual proficiency exam, with the added incentive of a cup presented by the two officers for the signaller who attained the highest aggregate.

Colour Party of the 1st Battalion ready for the parade and inspection by Maj.-Gen. A.E. Wardrop CB, CMG, General Officer Commanding North China Command at the Shanghai Racecourse, 18 February 1929.

'Eyes right': men of B Company, 1st Battalion, under Capt. B.E. King march past in the remarkable sight of General Salute for the GOC North China Command parade, 18 February 1929.

Men of the 1st Battalion fall in with kit bags to board the SS *Neuralia* sailing from Shanghai for Bombay, 14 November 1929. They stayed in India, their Foreign Service station, until the outbreak of the Second World War.

A Company, 1st Battalion, under Capt. M.D. Jephson, seated centre at Solon, India, 1930. Each company of the 1st Battalion was divided up for the hot season. The battalion was gathered together every two weeks, however, for 'khud' – climbing the hills. After a roll call at the highest point prizes were given for the first three back to the Guard Room. This stood the battalion in good stead and fitness when it was sent to Waziristan to quell the insurgent tribesmen.

Full Military Honours Funeral for Maj. E.T. 'Johnny' Horner MC, 1st Battalion, who died of natural causes at the British Military Hospital on 24 June 1931 aged forty-six. He was a popular character of the regiment, keen on polo and organiser of hunts even in the most exotic of climes that the regiment visited. His memorial stone was erected by his mother and brother officers.

1st Battalion Running Team, winners of the 1931 Lahore District Cross Country Cup, 1932. Standing, left to right: Ptes Hemmingway, Wingrove, Burton, Punyer, Lux, Coulston, Nugent. Seated: L-Cpl Nicholls, Pte Spaul, Lt Barclay, L-Cpl Desborough, Pte Whitmey.

Officers, warrant officers and sergeants sit behind the Battalion Colours at Swingate Camp, Dover, 1933. The comradeship of those who remained in the ranks of the Territorial Army after the First World War was closer than ever, and because of the unprecedented practical experience of these men, those who subsequently joined received the best training that the volunteer home forces saw until the Second World War.

The Officers' Dining Room, Norfolk Territorials' Summer Camp at Roedean, near Brighton, 1934. Behind the table is Arthur 'Poshie' Barnard, the Mess Sergeant (a position he held for over twenty years) with attendant mess waiters in their distinctive white jackets either side. The table looks a magnificent sight, highly polished along with the battalion's silver, laid out with military precision, and gleaming glasses. The scene is completed by the battalion's Colours at the end of the table.

Other ranks' kitchen and cooks all polished up ready for inspection at Territorial Camp, Dover, 1935. Cooks were not selected for what was often a thankless job so much on account of their culinary abilities, but '. . . rather because their presence on parade was not calculated to contribute to the smartness of the battalion in general'.

'All Aboard!' Territorial sergeants, all polished up in walking out dress, are ready for a trip to Dover on a charabanc from their summer camp at Swingate, 1935.

Band of the 2nd Battalion, accompanied by their CO, Lt-Col. R.H. Brundell-Bruce DSO on board HMS *Norfolk* when she was docked at Devonport, 1931. This was a fortuitous meeting as the 2nd Battalion had only recently occupied Raglan Barracks in the town, and was able to visit the 'old friend' of the regiment. Progress of HMS *Norfolk* was regularly reported in the 'Britannia' Regimental Journal.

2nd Battalion trooping their colours at Raglan Barracks, Devonport on 23 February 1934, to commemorate the 'Crossing of the Shumran Bend' on 23 February 1917. The battalion, having furnished five guards under the overall command of Lt-Col. Shand MC, march past Vice-Admiral E.J.A. Fullerton KCB, DSO, MA, Commander in Chief, Plymouth Station, taking the General Salute as the guards march past to their regimental march, 'Rule Britannia' in slow time.

Beating the retreat, Drums of the 1st Battalion in Jhansi, India 1935. The composition of the drums is worthy of note: the front rank are all tenor drums, a rare feature for any line infantry regiment, second and third ranks are side drums, and the fourth is bass drum and cymbals followed by flutes.

A very proud day for the band of the 2nd Battalion as they lead the parade of veterans of the Regimental Association past the Cenotaph in London, 24 May 1936.

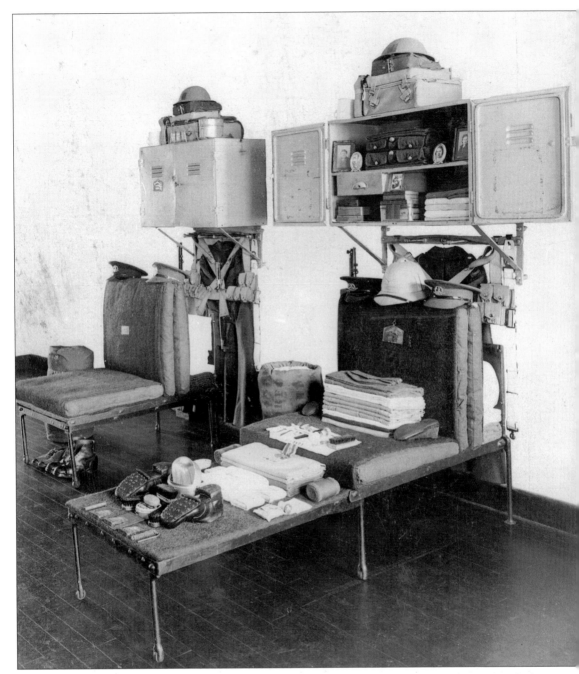

Prescribed method of kit lay-out for 2nd Battalion daily inspection while they were stationed in Gibraltar, 1937–9. The routine is remembered by many pre-war veterans of all battalions: all brasses polished front and back, blankets and spare uniforms blocked, all studs present on the soles of the boots; everything had to be 'just so' otherwise the whole lot could be pitched on to the floor with a flip of the Orderly Sergeant's cane with the words 'Get it sorted!' or simply 'Do it again'.

Officers of the 2nd Battalion at Gibraltar, 1938. Standing, left to right: Lt Gordon, 2nd Lt Hutchinson, Lt Grant, 2nd Lt Cooper-Key, 2nd Lt Holden, Lt Ridsdale, 2nd Lt Jickling, 2nd Lt Hallett, Lt Forte, 2nd Lt Brown. Seated: Capts Conder, Richardson, Cubitt, Maj. Prattley, Capts Marshall, Elwes and Barclay.

Depot Staff, 1938. Back row, left to right: CSM Burrows, Capt. Wilkinson, Lt Turner-Cain, Capt. Charlton, RSM Clarke. Front row: Maj. Stayner (Staff), Maj.-Gen. A.M. Lubbock CB, CMG, DSO (Commander 54th East Anglian Division and East Anglia Area), Maj. de Wilton, Maj. Wisdom. DC, RE.

Officer, Warrant Officers, NCOs and men in possession of the Long Service and Good Conduct medal at the Depot, 1938. Back row, left to right: Sgt W. Nobes, Sgt A. Playford, Pte H. Dawson, Pte W. Lansdowne, Cpl J. Quantrill, Sgt M. Lovett, Sgt H. Huggins. Front row: Capt. (QM) G. James, RSM G. Clarke, RQMS G. Cripps, QMS T. Reynolds MM, CSM L. Burrows, CQMS C. Jones, Sgt T. Billings.

Major de Wilton with VIP visitors at Britannia Barracks, 1939. The Earl of Munster, General the Viscount Gort VC, CIGS, Viscount Coke, the Earl of Airlie inspected the depot and observed the troops in training. As Chief of the Imperial General Staff, General Gort inspected many line infantry regiments on the immediate run up to the war, no doubt to ensure he 'had the best men for the best job'. Gort was to be Commander-in-Chief of the British Expeditionary Force in France later that year.

THE SECOND WORLD WAR

HM King George VI, Colonel-in-Chief, the Royal Norfolk Regiment, accompanied by Lt-Col. J.H. Jewson MC, TD, inspecting members of the 4th Battalion at Gorleston, as part of his tour of the East Coast Defences, 23 August 1940.

Officers of the 1st Battalion, Bangalore, India, 1940. Back row, left to right: 2nd Lts Gudgin, Whitworth, Bagwell, Fisher, Burton, Robertson, Baker, Beck, Lilly, Atkinson, Ferrier, Woodhouse, Cooper-Key. Front row: Lt (QM) Grix, Lt Darby, Capt. Packard, Maj. Fitzgerald, Maj. Drake-Briscoe, Lt-Col. G.C. Thorne (Officer Commanding), Lt Brinkley (Adjt), Capt. Freeman-Taylor, Lt Lewis, 2nd Lt Hamond, 2nd Lt Holden.

Militia recruits messing 11 a.m. tea at Britannia Barracks, 1939. This was a somewhat misleading title as they were the first conscripted servicemen of the Second World War. Part of a national intake of 35,000 men, they were recruited under the 1939 Military Training Act. Upon reaching twenty-one men were to undergo six months' military training in one of the three services, followed by three and a half in the Reserve, during which time they might be recalled in an emergency for full-time duty. Subsequently they were destined to serve a good deal longer than six months.

Under the watchful eye of the physical training instructors recruits combine teamwork and fitness, essential to training, on the poles in front of Britannia Barracks, autumn 1939.

Training recruits in use of the .303 Short Magazine Lee Enfield Rifles before their first time on the outside range at Britannia Barracks, autumn 1939. Because of the influx of recruits, uniforms were piecemeal as in 1914; equipment was a strange mix of 1908 pattern webbing, First World War rifles and 1930s working fatigue overalls.

Officers and men of the Headquarters 70th (Young Serviceman) Battalion, Taverham Hall, near Norwich, 1940. Seated centre is the Battalion's Commanding Officer Lt-Col. E. Thistleton-Smith, and seated second from right is their ex-guardsman, RSM Swingler.

On the drive near their camp at Taverham Hall men of the 70th (Young Serviceman) Battalion are blanket shaking, June 1941. This enabled their instruction in the making of 'bed blocks', part of the daily routine of kit layout and inspection in regular army life.

Men of the 70th (Young Serviceman) Battalion in a trench with fixed bayonets ready to go 'over the top' preparatory to bayonet fighting practice, Taverham Hall, June 1940.

A happy quintet of young soldiers, aged between eighteen and twenty, who seem to be enjoying their training at Taverham Hall, June 1940. When fully trained they would be drafted to one of the active service battalions. In the summer of 1943 the 70th Battalions which had been set up in most regiments of the British Army were disbanded but not without furnishing thousands of well-trained and keen men to active battalions, this training avoiding many of the tragedies of young men in action a generation before.

Officers of the 7th Battalion, 1939. Standing, left to right: 2nd Lts Gibson, Wood, McDonnell, Lt Hoghton, 2nd Lts McKenzie, Thorneycroft, Jamieson, Barrett, Gill, Rought, Brand, Smith, Colley, Bett, King. Seated: Capt. Hinsley (Chaplain), Capt. Allen, Capt. Kershaw, Maj. Wilson, Maj. Stourton MP, Lt-Col C.A. Debenham, Capts Jickling, Wilkin, Hawkins, Lt Reynolds MM (QM), Lt Monteuuis RAMC.

General Georges inspects a Guard of Honour of the 2nd Battalion at Marchiennes, early 1940. Following their mobilisation at Aldershot in 1939, the 2nd Battalion left for France aboard the vessels *Royal Daffodil* and *Royal Sovereign*, arriving at Cherbourg on 21 September 1939 – the first complete infantry unit of the BEF to land.

Capt. Peter Barclay and L-Cpl Mick Davis are congratulated by comrades in the 2nd Battalion following the announcement of their awards of the Military Cross and Military Medal after their gallantry in a successful patrol into enemy lines on 4 January 1940. These were the very first gallantry decorations for the British Expeditionary Force, and indeed the British Army, in the Second World War.

CSM George Gristock VC. He enlisted in March 1919 into the Dragoon Guards and transferred to 2nd Battalion, Royal Norfolk Regiment, in 1935. Working his way up the ranks he was promoted WO II in the field on 20 May 1940. A day later, near the River Escant, south of Tournai, the enemy breached his company's right flank after a prolonged attack. Detailing eight riflemen to give covering fire, he advanced under heavy fire and, although badly wounded in both legs, he gained an undetected fire position and successfully silenced the machine-gun position which had inflicted so many casualties on his company. He dragged himself back to the right flank and would not leave until contact with the battalion had been restored. Evacuated back to England he died of his wounds in hospital at Brighton on 16 July 1940. He was awarded the Victoria Cross, gazetted 23/8/40, the first to the regiment in the Second World War. It was later presented to the Regimental Museum by his parents where it may be seen today.

About 1600 hrs, 2nd Battalion HQ, Le Paradis, 27 May 1940, painted by John Willis. One of the most horrible and tragic episodes in the history of the Royal Norfolk Regiment took place on this day when over ninety men of the 2nd Battalion, many wounded, battle fatigued and over-run, surrendered to No. 4 Company, 1st Battalion, 2nd SS 'Totenkopf' Regiment at Le Paradis. Marched down the road and driven into a meadow, they were marched along a barn wall where two German machine-guns opened fire massacring the men. Incredibly two Privates, Albert Pooley and Bill O'Callaghan, although wounded, ,survived. Eventually returning home, they fought on in a battle to be believed, and finally brought the SS Officer responsible, Fritz Knochlein, to a war crimes trial. Found guilty, he was hanged in 1949. By the end of the Dunkirk evacuation, for which the 2nd Battalion was part of the force providing the rear guard, only 5 officers and 134 soldiers returned to England, from a battalion over a thousand strong: the rest were taken prisoner of war or were lying in the fields of France forever.

Sergeants of the 2nd Battalion in 1941. Back row, left to right: L-Sgt Davies MM, Sgts White, Everett, Allison, Belmont, Bond, Wiley, Wells. Second row: Sgts Bastard, Collings, Harford, L-Sgt Gaze, Sgts Edgecombe, Cook, Nichols, L-Sgt Clegg. Third row: Sgts Huckvale, Adams, Lake, L-Sgt Walton, Sgts Hall, Pitchers, Taylor, Barratt, L-Sgt Wood. Fourth row: CSM Derry, C-Sgts Dean, Jones, Clitheroe, Keeble, Collop, Thornton, Sgt Palmer, ORQMS Briggs. Seated: CSMs Firmin, Slaughter, Milne, Capt Twidle (Adjt), Lt-Col. Winter, RSM Wright, Maj. Allen, CSM Utting, RQMS Goldsmith. Seated on grass: Sgt Miller RAOC attached, Sgts Cassidy, Street, Atkins.

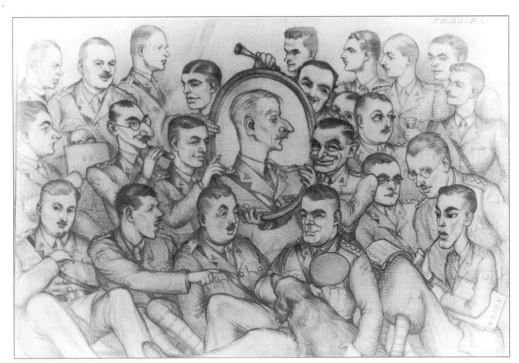

A cartoon of all the officers of the 4th Battalion signed and presented to Arthur 'Poshie' Barnard along with a silver cigarette case upon his retirement from the 4th Battalion in 1941, after over thirty years in the Norfolk Territorial Battalions, many of them as Mess Sergeant to the 4th Battalion.

Men of the 4th Battalion take part in an assault on a pillbox during manoeuvres at Great Yarmouth, while they were based there on coastal defence duty, 31 July to 2 August 1940.

Men of the 6th Battalion manning a road blockade open it to let a Bren Gun carrier through on Cromer Road, Sheringham, October 1940. The Battle of Britain had been fought in the skies but the fear of invasion was still very much in everybody's mind during the 1940–1 winter; beaches were still closed and the whole coastline was an area of restricted movement, much of it controlled by the Territorial soldiers of the Royal Norfolk Regiment.

A Company, 4th Battalion at Duckworth Mill, Blackburn, 1941. Having weathered one of the worst winters on record on coastal defence duties in Norfolk, the men of the 4th, 5th and 6th Battalion were plummeted to the other end of the scale into the sweltering heat of Johore and Singapore, fighting a new war and a new enemy. They fought 'like Bengal Tigers' but were forced back to Singapore where the forces were surrendered to the Japanese by Gen. Alexander; many men of the 18th Division wanted to fight on. Their greatest fight was to come in enduring their captivity in Japanese hands, many of them on the infamous Burma–Siam 'Railway of Death'.

Men of Attleborough Company, Ninth Battalion, Norfolk Home Guard, *c.* 1941. Originally the Local Defence Volunteers when first raised in May 1940, within two weeks 30,000 local men had volunteered for service in Norfolk. The Home Guard comprised mainly men too young or too old for military service, and those unfit or employed in War Reserved Occupations; it was keenly supported throughout the war. Norfolk had raised seventeen Battalions by the time the Home Guard was stood down in 1944.

Wroxham and Ormesby Broads flotilla, November 1940. When scares of invasion were at their highest even the Broads were patrolled to guard against invasion landings from seaplanes. The boats, originally pleasure craft, were requisitioned and fitted with Lewis Guns manned by men of local Home Guard units and men of the 70th (Young Soldier) Battalion, Royal Norfolk Regiment. The flotilla was under the command of Commander B. Youatt RN, part of 2nd Corps, 213th Bde 18th (sdv) Division.

Home Guard exercises were frequent, and although usually well improvised they were often a source of amusement for the locals. Here some men of Sheringham Home Guard Battalion stand ready to deal with any of the crew from the 'tank' which has just crashed into their tank trap after they bombed it with a 'Molotov cocktail', November 1940.

The team of Norfolk Home Guardsmen seated proudly behind their Blacker Bombard and Aircraft Lewis machine guns (modified for use by ground troops), runners up in the Norfolk and Cambridgeshire District Home Guard Battle Platoon Competition (Second Series) held at Brandon Battle Area, 30 April 1944.

Women of the 40th Norfolk Company ATS, Britannia Barracks, *c.* 1940. Raised in the autumn of 1938, the battalion rapidly grew under the energetic leadership of Mrs Barclay of Colney Hall. The women underwent similar training to the men, from PT to firing on the rifle range. Their main function, however, was to back up and help administrate the Regimental Depot which became the Royal Norfolk Regiment Training Centre under the command of Lt-Col. N.P. Shand MC. Their jobs ranged from cooks to clerks and drivers to motor pool workers, many of them posted to back up fighting units. Lt-Col. Shand said of them: 'The 40th did take their place in their County Regiments' traditions: they might have been one of the old companies; the harder the work the more cheerful they all were; nothing was too much bother, no time was too long at work, they were a credit to the badge of Britannia they all wore with such pride.'

After PT men of the 7th Battalion form up for the camera at Bacton, 1941. The 7th Battalion had practically been annihilated during the retreat to Dunkirk in 1940; only thirty men and one officer returned home in 1940. The battalion was reconstructed with an initial cadre of 18 officers and 150 men in late 1940. Initially based in the Grimsby area, their training was completed in Norfolk when they returned to the training areas of North Walsham, Bacton and Sidestrand in 1941.

Band of the 1st Battalion, 1944. During their station on Wimbledon Common, they were part of the 'Thin Brown Line' for the Defence of London. When the battalion was part of the 24th Guard's Independent Brigade Group, the band's presence on Saturday Adjutant's Parades in London was thought in high quarters to be a close rival to the Guards' Depot Band. In war the band's role changed, with most of the members becoming battalion stretcher bearers.

A programme for Norwich's 'Salute the Soldier' Week, 10–17 June 1944. The city's aim was to raise £1,000,000 to equip the Royal Norfolk Regiment through fund raising events ranging from exhibitions, displays, dances and band concerts to a Grand Parade of all services through Norwich. The people of Norfolk's support and pride in their county regiment never faltered. 'Salute the Soldier' weeks were held across Norfolk in major towns and groups of smaller parishes, every one raising more than their set target.

A-Cpl Sidney 'Basher' Bates VC. A true cockney, 'Basher' joined the 1st Battalion when it was stationed in London in 1941. Landing on D-Day with them, two months later, on 6 August 1944, near Sourdeval when the enemy was threatening a major breakthrough into his company's area, he seized a Bren gun and charged through a hail of bullets and, although wounded from the mortar bombs falling around him, he picked himself up twice and carried on his advance: the enemy began to withdraw. A third shell injured him mortally but he kept on firing until his strength failed him. Despite being removed from the field rapidly after he fell by L-Cpl Ernie Seaman, 'Basher' died of his wounds two days later. For his singular example and gallantry he was awarded the Victoria Cross, gazetted on 2/12/44.

Major David Auldgo Jamieson VC. Commissioned into the 5th Battalion in May 1939 at the outbreak of war he joined the 7th Battalion in 1939. Granted a Regular Commission in 1941, he proceeded with the 7th in June 1944 as 2 I/C 'D' Company. On 7/8 August 1944, south of Grimbosq, Captain Jamieson's company established a bridgehead over the River Orne. Suffering a barrage of attacks over thirty-six hours he constantly demonstrated superb leadership and great personal bravery. Often the situation seemed hopeless but was restored by his personal coolness and determination. He was the only member of the Royal Norfolk Regiment to live to receive his Victoria Cross, gazetted 26/10/44.

1st Battalion Carriers at Tinchebray, August 1944. Following the Battle of Sourdevalle the battalion rested at Tinchebray, and recovered some of its losses when it was joined by 7 officers and 160 other ranks of the 7th Battalion, this being most of the men left of that battalion after its heavy losses at Epron and Orne.

Capt. Oakley and Lt Buckerfield examining maps at Asten, Holland, shortly before the advance and liberation of Helmond by the 1st Battalion on 26 September 1944.

Men of the 1st Battalion listening to the radio and examining maps for that night's patrols, making the best of a bitter winter on the front lines in Venraij, Holland, November 1944.

Men of C Company, 1st Battalion during a break on the march to Wassnum, 26 November 1944.

Men of the 1st Battalion enter Wassnum, having left Oostrum, November 1944. They went on to engage in the dangerous clearance of buildings throughout the town. They were to spend the rest of 1944 in Holland in what seemed like constant patrolling and training for the amphibious crossing of the Maas.

Capt. A. Dines of London with his Salvation Army Mobile Canteen, Holland, December 1945, serving men of C Company – observed by Maj. S.T. Mercer (centre) and Capt. J.B. Dye (right).

Photographed shortly before the Battalion entered Germany in February 1945, these are men of 17 Platoon D Company, 1st Battalion. Back row, left to right: Cole, Maddox, Johnson, Wright, Deacon, Plumb, Slater. Middle row: Rose, Dodd, Peacock, Porrett, Smith, Spruce, Clabburn. Front row: Young, Blackmore, L-Cpl Haines, L-Cpl Gould, Sgt Rust, Cpl Carter, L-Cpl Vincent, L-Cpl Hook.

Men of D Company, 1st Battalion in Bremen, 27 April 1945. Following the heavy toll of the final big push through Kervenheim, Lingen and Brinkum the final major battle fought by the 1st Battalion was for Bremen on 26 April 1945; the Reich was on its last legs and German soldiers were constantly surrendering. This battle was soon won with a few drinks after at Becks Brewery!

T-Cpt. John Neil 'Jack' Randle VC. He was commissioned from OCTU into the Royal Norfolk Regiment early in 1940 and proceeded to the 2nd Battalion in April of the same year. During the attack on 'Norfolk Bunker', Kohima, Assam between 6 May 1944 he led an attack. Almost immediately the company was held up by machine-gun fire from an enemy bunker but Captain Randle charged it single-handedly. Although mortally wounded he threw his grenade into the bunker and threw his body with his last energy over the slit and sealed it completely. His selfless gallantry earned him the Victoria Cross, gazetted 12/12/44.

The Viceroy of India, Field Marshal The Viscount Wavell decorating L-Cpl W. Williams of the 2nd Battalion with the Military Medal for his outstanding gallantry at GPT Ridge, where he accounted for seventeen Japanese single-handedly. The ceremony took place on Imphal airstrip, December 1944.

Men of the 2nd Battalion cross the Irrawaddy by DUKW and disembark at the bridgehead at Ngazun, Burma, February 1945.

Muleteers of the 2nd Battalion keeping their mules in trim on the airstrip, 'Rotten Row', Burma, 1944.

Lieutenant George Arthur Knowland VC, Royal Norfolk Regiment, attained No. 1 Commando. Leading a forward platoon they came under heavy fire, 300 Japanese concentrating on his 24 men. His forward Bren crew were all killed or badly wounded so he went forward to man it himself, standing up to fire at 10 yards range until the casualties had been evacuated. For 12 hours he held his ground until mortally wounded. He was wearing his Britannia Cap badge to the last. He was awarded the last Victoria Cross to the Regiment, gazetted on 12 April 1945. The Royal Norfolk Regiment was awarded five Victoria Crosses, a total unsurpassed by any other county regiment during the Second World War.

Lt-Col. Wilkins seated in the centre with his dress side hat on smiles proudly with the men of the 2nd Battalion, India, 1945. Having gone through the whole Far Eastern war from the sieges of Kohima and Imphal to the crossing of the Irrawaddy, the men of the 2nd Battalion had distinguished themselves and been a complete credit to the regiment, acquitting themselves with more individual decorations than any other Battalion in the 2nd Division throughout the campaign.

Field-Marshal Montgomery decorates CSM Tom Catlin with the Military Medal for his gallantry on 6 August 1944, when during the Battle of Sourdeval (despite the rest of his company HQ being wiped out) he stuck by his post until he was able to reach a friendly tank to direct its fire on to the German tank causing the damage; while informing the tank commander they received a direct hit in which the CSM was badly wounded. Brought back to the Regimental Aid Post, on his way he passed through Battalion Headquarters to see the CO to give him the situation of his company area. CSM Catlin's citation states: 'His services to his battalion during this attack can hardly be equalled in this campaign.'

1st Battalion sergeants, June 1945. Back row, left to right: Sgts Franks, Reeve, Thomas, Savidge, Smart, Webb, Rust, Shaw, Slapp, Toll. Fourth row: Sgts Staind, Boyles, Collins, Bennett, Stocker, Addison, Nelson, Roff, Newman, Johnson. Third row: Sgts Loades, Percival, Ming, Marshall, Kerrison, Smith, Weldon, Kay MM, Paskell, Hilling. Second row: CQMSs Howard, Ellis, Sgts Allen, Heathcote, Pegg, Barleycorn MM, Bambridge, Graveg, Brown, Williams, CQMS Lacey. Front row: CSMs Langford DCM, Flint, Wilkinson, RSM Brown, L-Col. F.P. Barclay DSO, MC, Capt. R.C. Wilson MC, CSMs Brown, Catlin MM, Fuller.

Marshal Georgi Zhukov, the Soviet Union's foremost military commander in the Second World War, congratulates the commander of the British Section Guard of Honour, provided entirely from men of the 1st Battalion, paraded for his visit to the combined allied forces occupying the Rhineland, 10 June 1945.

Some of the men of the 4th, 5th and 6th Battalions on Bangkok airfield about to board the plane to take them home, September 1945. The highest number of casualties incurred by the Royal Norfolk Regiment in the Second World War was in the Far Eastern War, mostly from the depraved and inhuman treatment of men while prisoners of war in Japanese hands. Up to 70 per cent of the three battalions never returned.

Men representing all battalions of the Royal Norfolk Regiment parade in front of Norwich City Hall when the Regiment was granted the Freedom of the City (the right to march through it '. . . with bayonets fixed, colours flying and bands playing') on 3 October 1945. The Guard of Honour was commanded by Maj. David Jamieson VC, with colours carried by Lt John Lincoln MC and Capt. Ernest Ridger, with the Guard Detachments commanded by Maj. J.B. Dye MC, Capt. R.F. Howard MBE, Maj. B. Savory and Capt. E.T. Gibbons respectively.

Contingent of men representing all Battalions of the Royal Norfolk Regiment for the Victory March through London, June 1946. Back row, left to right: Cpl Yowell, L-Cpl Kindred, Pte Poxon, Cpl Lee, Pte Hillings, L-Cpl Wones, Pte Davies. Second row: Ptes Hanscombe, Barker, Andrews, Cpl Aldous, Pte Stonelake, Cpl Mace, Pte Ainsworth. Front row: Lt McArthur (King's Colour), Sgts Buckenham, Forrest, C-Sgt Rudling, Maj. H.R. Holden MC, C-Sgt Driscoll, Sgt Daniels, Sgt Evans.

THE NATIONAL SERVICE YEARS
& THE END OF AN ERA

A young National Serviceman reporting to the gate is given directions by a Regimental Policeman at Britannia Barracks, c. 1955. Conscription was retained after 1945 to meet Britain's worldwide defence and peace-keeping commitments. The 1948 National Service Act made every male citizen aged between eighteen and twenty-six (certain skilled workers and students could defer) liable for eighteen months' compulsory military service, with four years in reserve. In 1950 this changed to two years, with three and a half in reserve.

Percy Mark Herbert, Bishop of Norwich, dedicates the new Colours presented to the 1st Battalion by Lt-General Sir Richard L. McCreery KCB, KBE, DSO, MC, GOC, British Army of the Rhine on behalf of King George VI, at Neuhaus, Germany, 7 November 1946. The old Colours, originally presented by King Edward VII at Buckingham Palace in 1909, had travelled with the battalion in England, Ireland, West Indies, Egypt, Shanghai, India and Germany on their campaigns for almost forty years. They were paraded for the last time immediately before the dedication of the new Colours, and marched off to the band playing 'Auld Lang Syne'.

Parade on the occasion of the laying up of the old Colours of the 1st Battalion at Sandringham, 29 June 1947. Maj. W.A. Adderson DSO, commanding the Guard of Honour, accompanies King George VI, Colonel-in-Chief, as he inspects the guard of hand-picked men selected from the 1st Battalion, stationed in Germany and sent over to represent the battalion on this special occasion. Guard Sergeant-Major, the right-hand marker for the parade, is CSM Ted Shepherd MM.

The 4th Battalion (TA) parades its Colours, which had been lodged at Britannia Barracks for the duration of the war, for the first time on 30 June 1947. The Lord Mayor takes the salute as they march past Norwich City Hall, exercising the regiment's newly earned right to march through the city with fixed bayonets and bands playing.

Farewell parade to General Sir E.P. Strickland KCB, KBE, CMG, DSO, JP, Colonel of the Regiment, at Britannia Barracks, 26 February 1946. Main group, left to right: Lt-Col. H.S. Hewick (The Dorset Regiment), Maj.-Gen. H.P.M. Berney-Ficklin CB, MC, Gen. Sir E.P. Strickland, Lt-Col. Freeman-Taylor, OC 4th Battalion. General Strickland joined The Norfolk Regiment from the Militia in 1888 and progressed up the ranks, serving in Burma, Dongola and Egypt. He was wounded twice during the First World War. After a distinguished career he was appointed Colonel of the Regiment in December 1917, a position he held for twenty-seven years. After taking the salute and an emotional farewell his position was taken by Maj.-Gen. H.P.M. Berney-Ficklin CB, MC, a fine officer with a long and distinguished career. His immediate post-war duties had included sitting in Presidence of the War Crimes trials for Belsen, the Nazi death camp.

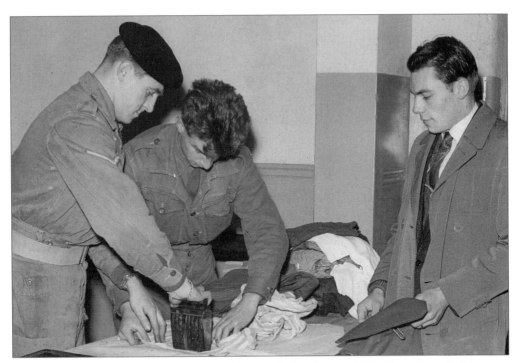

A new serviceman reports to the Quartermaster's Store to be kitted out, *c.* 1950. His uniform piled at the top of the table is being stamped with his army number by the supervising corporal, no doubt with the eight digit 22800000 series. Each man's number was not only indelibly marked on all his clothes but also on his mind!

Major Robert Hamond, Officer Commanding the Depot (seated centre), presides over another intake of National Servicemen at Britannia Barracks, *c.* 1950. Intakes into the Royal Norfolk Regiment would be in blocks averaging about seventy men every one or two months, divided into two platoons; two intakes would train in tandem. Each of the platoons was named after the posthumous Victoria Cross winners of the Second World War: Gristock, Randle, Bates and Knowland.

Depot RSM Bert 'Winkie' Fitt DCM, 1959. The undoubted 'voice of the parade ground', his presence was legendary, no doubt remembered by all those who were drilled by him or served under his command. He joined The Norfolk Regiment in January 1933 at Britannia Barracks, and was awarded his DCM for his 'conspicuous bravery and command of a critical situation' during the assault on 'Norfolk' bunker (the same action for which Captain 'Jack' Randle was posthumously awarded his VC) during the Battle of Kohima in 1944. He completed his service in 1960 with a terminal grant of £1,061 and a pension of £6 15s a week.

Gristock Platoon, March 1958, in the gym at Britannia Barracks. Here the 'man in the street' was put through his paces, along with the arduous cross-country running, to produce a physically fit man ready for military training.

Soldiers of the Recruit Training Battalion putting the newly issued FN FAL rifle through its paces, February 1958.

Recruit Training Battalion Bren Gun crews dash into action during a training exercise on Mousehold Heath, 1958.

Men of anti-tank platoon, Germany 1957. Left to right: Pte Taylor, L-Cpl Docherty (REME), L-Cpl Jordan (looking over gun shield) and L-Cpl Spooner.

One of the rooms in the original Regimental Museum, Cameron House, Britannia Barracks, March 1951. Every soldier was encouraged to learn and be familiar with his regimental history, to understand what the badge he wore stood for and why he should take pride in the Battle Honours emblazoned on the Colours.

Weekly pay parade at Britannia Barracks in 1959. At the time when this picture was taken, after six months' service the basic pay for a regular soldier was 91s and for a national serviceman 38s 6d a week. Regular corporals earned 112s, sergeants 182s and 29s a day for a newly commissioned officer.

NAAFI break at Britannia Barracks, c. 1959. The universal meeting place to have a snack, a drink, a rest and to socialise in camps and barracks across the world was the NAAFI (Navy, Army and Air Forces Industries). Established in 1921, their job was to supply part of the messing goods of HM Forces and to organise service entertainment, returning all surplus funds to the forces either in cash rebates, discounts or amenities.

Final inspection at a passing out parade of National Servicemen, Britannia Barracks, *c.* 1952. National Service intakes ended on 31 December 1960, the last of the conscripts leaving the army in May 1963. It is worthy of note that National Servicemen had a one in two chance of being posted overseas into Active Service Zones. Serving in Malaya, Cyprus, Kenya and Korea (where National Servicemen formed 10 per cent of the whole British contingent), many National Servicemen died fighting in these all too forgotten wars in the uneasy 'peace' since the end of the Second World War.

Brigadier W.J. O'Daunt CBE, Colonel of the Regiment, seated centre, with the warrant officers and sergeants of the 1st Battalion gathered together for 'Almanza Day', Berlin, 1950. This was a major anniversary for the regiment. The Battle of Almanza took place on 25 April 1707, during the War of Spanish Succession, and although a defeat the 9th Foot then distinguished themselves. For their gallantry on that day the 9th Foot were awarded the Figure of Britannia as their emblazoned badge by Queen Anne.

Winter Line, looking towards .169 across the Samichon Valley from part of the area occupied by the 1st Battalion, 1951. Having left England on 30 August 1951 on the SS *Empire Orwell*, the 1st Battalion was engaged in Korea. The battalion survived a perishingly cold winter, and saw tough campaigning and violent skirmishes, defending lines and valleys. Korea was the last Battle Honour of the Royal Norfolk Regiment and like all the others it was hard won. Battalion casualties had not been light, 1 Officer and 32 soldiers killed, 10 officers and 98 wounded, 1 officer and 5 men posted missing. The 1st Battalion left Korea for Hong Kong on 28 September 1952.

Having docked the previous night, some men of the 1st Battalion pause for the camera at Liverpool Docks on 6 October 1954, having disembarked from the troopship *Devonshire* upon their return from three years' service in the Far East.

Some of the 450 officers and men of the 1st Battalion march past City Hall in sixes as Lt-Col. Sir Edmund Bacon Bt, OBE, TD, Her Majesty's Lord Lieutenant of Norfolk, takes the salute on the occasion of the Battalion's 'Welcome Home' from Korea Parade on 15 December 1954. Marching for one of the last occasions with 'bayonets fixed and bands playing', applauded by crowds along the route, they proceeded to a special service in their honour at Norwich Cathedral.

The grand 'Welcome Home' celebrations of 15 December 1954 were completed in Norwich with a luncheon for the officers and men of the 1st Battalion, who enjoyed oxtail soup, roast turkey, plum pudding, cheese and biscuits. The luncheon was given by the councils of Norfolk, Norwich and Great Yarmouth at the Samson and Hercules, Tombland.

Patrolling a typical street, Cyprus, 1955. After barely a year of home service in Colchester the 1st Battalion left for Cyprus from RAF Lyneham in eighteen Hastings aircraft on Monday 17 October 1955. For the next twelve months they were engaged in a campaign similar to that experienced by the regiment over the years in Ireland; a period of cordon and search, curfew enforcement, crowd control armed with batons and tear gas, bombs thrown in dark alleys or under jeeps. No chances could be taken with the EOKA terrorists.

Lt-Col. W.H. Brinkley and his escort outside MILPOL, Limassol, Cyprus, January 1956.

'Nothing like a cooler.' Humour is an essential part of survival in service life in peace and war, here a few laughs are shared at the Bell Hotel, a marquee where the soft drink licensee is Sgt A. 'Dinger' Bell, Nicosia, Cyprus, 1956.

Cheers! Men of the 1st Battalion welcomed home on Thorpe station Norwich on their return from Cyprus, 13 December 1956. After docking at Liverpool two special trains left, one for London and the other for Norwich, taking the majority of men home. The men arriving in Norwich were greeted by families and officially by the Lord Mayor, Mr Arthur South, on Thorpe station, as well as being suitably plied with beer, sandwiches and buns, supplied free by local firms and distributed by ladies of the WVS and Civil Defence Welfare.

Combined exercise of the 4th Battalion, Royal Norfolk Regiment (TA) and the 4th Battalion Suffolk Regiment (TA), Stanford 'Stanta' Battle Area, 1950. Against a typical Breckland background another reconnoitring party with their carrier go forward.

An outpost of men of the 4th Battalion equipped with Vickers machine gun and rifles, ready to hold their ground! Left to right: Sgt Barr, Cpl Hutson, Pte Ketteringham of Norwich and Pte Cross of Thetford.

'Spread out in line formation', a 'flushing out exercise'. Left to right: 4th Suffolk man attached, Pte Newton, Pte Barham, Sgt Hawes, Ptes Underwood, Reeder, Palmer, Sgt Hunt.

Ready for the final advance, awaiting orders. Left to right: Pte Bailey with 2-in mortar, Pte Harmer, attached 4th Suffolk, CSM Paskell, Pte Reeder, attached 4th Suffolk, Cpl Taylor.

Officers 4th Battalion TA, Shorncliffe, June 1951. Back row, left to right: 2nd Lts Raywood, Payne, Harper, Lt Weeks TD, 2nd Lts Clarke, Prior. Middle row: Lts Boulton, Hunter, Capt. Brittain RAMC, Capts Howard, Burdett, Rutter TD, Hornor, Peacock, Lt Herbert. Front row: Maj. (QM) Reynolds MM, TD, Maj. Breach, Maj. Summerfield, Lt-Col. Wilkins (OC), Capt. Power (Adjt), Maj. Cary-Elwes TD, Maj. Wright.

RSM J.A. Sewell of the 4th Battalion (TA) inspecting some of the scarlet tunics received at the Cattle Market drill hall, which were sent in response to the advert published in the *Eastern Daily Press* appealing for donations of such attire to outfit the battalion band for the special parades in 1952, the Coronation year.

Queen Elizabeth the Queen Mother compliments Maj. S.S.F. Hornor on the turnout and drill of the Guard of Honour after she shared a few words with CSM 'Dutchy' Everson of A Company, 4th Battalion (TA). The Guard of Honour was supplied by the battalion on the occasion of Her Majesty's acceptance of the Freedom of King's Lynn on 26 July 1954.

Her Majesty the Queen, accompanied by Capt. R. Boulton, inspects a Guard of Honour of the 4th Battalion in front of Norwich City Hall, Wednesday 3 July 1957, on her visit to the city. She visited the Royal Norfolk Show later that day.

Recruiting poster for Norfolk Home Guard, 1953. The first appeals to re-raise the Home Guard came during the Suez Crisis in 1952. It was well funded with Government money, well equipped, well armed and had a wealth of experienced members at its foundation. Sixteen battalions all across Norfolk were re-formed and trained. The support and enthusiasm so prevalent during the Second World War did not emerge in peacetime when England was not under direct threat, and despite early fervour the Home Guard was totally disbanded again in Norfolk by the end of the 1950s.

It didn't take long for the many ex-servicemen who joined the Norfolk Home Guard to get their eye in on the range, as pictured, *c.* 1953. To encourage rifle proficiency there was the hotly contested Home Guard East Anglian District Rifle Association Cup, run on a round sector knock-out basis at meetings held on the ranges at weekends.

Lt-Col. Robson OBE leads his men of the 15th Battalion, Norfolk Home Guard at the Remembrance Sunday Church Parade at Terrington St Clement, 7 November 1954.

One of the most emotional days in the history of the Royal Norfolk Regiment was the day the men bid farewell to the regimental flag, 29 August 1959. Following the Defence White Paper of April 1957, which announced that the number of units in the British Army must be reduced, a number of grand old county regiments were amalgamated. Among the first to receive this bitter blow was the Royal Norfolk Regiment, amalgamated with the Suffolk Regiment to create the 1st East Anglian Regiment. The closing service was held at Britannia Barracks, after which the retreat was sounded and the regimental flag was lowered for the last time.

The award winning band of the 4th Battalion (TA), October 1964. Territorial battalions of amalgamated units retained their identities with their old regiments, even after the creation of The Royal Anglian Regiment which amalgamated all the old line regiments of East Anglia from The Royal Leicesters to The Essex Regiment. Finally in 1967/8 Territorial Army Category III units, like the 4th Royal Norfolks, were ordered by the government of the day to disband; all that remained was a cadre of five officers and three other ranks, the last to serve under the Britannia Cap badge. In 1970 this cadre ceased to exist on the creation of A (Norfolk and Suffolk) Company 6th Battalion, Royal Anglian Regiment.

BOYS OF THE
OLD BRIGADE

RSM G. James welcomes ex-9th Foot and Norfolk Regiment Chelsea Pensioners. Left to right: W.J. Kerr (aged 72), J. Green (aged 73), A.C. Kiddell (aged 70), C. East (aged 71), E. Davey (aged 71) at the Regimental Reunion held at Colchester, Sunday 4 July 1926. The Norfolk Regiment Association was formed in 1922 to provide an organisation that by means of periodic meetings at homes, dances and reunions would keep alive the comradeship enjoyed during service in the regiment, and through association funds assist those who had fallen on difficult times.

King George V on an informal visit to the Regimental War Memorial Cottages when they were nearing completion, 2 February 1921. Left to right: Mrs Hadow, Maj. A.L. Hadow CMG (OC Depot), the Earl of Leicester, King George V, Queen Mary, Lt-Col G.J.B. Duff MC, Maj. R. Otter MC, the Princess Royal, Lt-Col. C.M. Jickling OBE.

Dignitaries including The Lord Lieutenant, the Bishop of Norwich, the Lord Mayor of Norwich and the Mayors of Yarmouth and King's Lynn at the opening of the twelve Regimental War Memorial Cottages, 11 August 1921. The cottages, erected totally by charitable subscription, were built as a memorial to The Norfolk Regiment's dead of the First World War, and provided twelve homes for disabled soldiers of the regiment.

Soldiers representing all battalions of the regiment gather after the formal unveiling of the memorial tablet at the Regimental War Memorial Cottages by the Lord Lieutenant of Norfolk, 11 August 1921. The memorial stone was erected in memory of the 6,000 officers and men who died serving with The Norfolk Regiment 1914–18.

Nearly 100 members of the 1/4th Battalion Old Comrades Association fall in behind serving men of A (MG) Company 4th Battalion (TA) at St Andrew's Hall ready to march to the Armistice Sunday Service at Norwich Cathedral, 1930.

Pte Charles Crampion, 2nd Battalion, won his first Distinguished Conduct Medal for gallantry in Tartan, Birmah on 4 May 1889. During the South African War he distinguished himself again, in action at Karee Siding on 29 March 1900 when he was injured while helping a wounded comrade – and recommended for a bar for his DCM. By some oversight he was presented with a second full size medal and later the bar he should have received in the first instance, thus making his medal group unique in the British Army.

Reunions and nostalgia are not only found when soldiers leave the army. Often groups would gather for the camera, such as men still serving with particular battalions after significant enlistment dates or who saw particular actions during the First World War. This is one of the most unusual as it shows the two battalions that were serving at the same place at the same time. They are the still serving survivors of the 'Norset' composite battalion, Mesopotamia, 4 February to 24 July 1916 at Aldershot, June 1927. (*Denotes Dorset Regiment.) Back row, left to right: Pte Radford*, Pte Palmer DCM*, Pte Hanham*, Pte Page, Pte Dummer*. Middle row: Cpl Buxton, L-Cpl Brighton, Pte Roberts*, L-Cpl Barber, Pte Brehant*, Pte Sewter, Pte Faulkner*, Cpl Nash. Seated: L-Sgt Houslow*, Sgt Noller, Capt. A.E. Hankins*, Maj. W. Clement DSO*, Capt E.L. Stephenson MC, Lt and Qmr Bolingbroke*, Sgt Lee*.

Veterans, Chelsea Pensioners and servicemen enjoy the London Branch of The Royal Norfolk Regimental Association Annual Dinner at Duke of Yorks Headquarters, King's Road, Chelsea, on the evening of 5 November 1954.

Reunion Dinner of the 1/6th (Cyclist) Battalion, King's Arms Hotel, North Walsham, 30 April 1960. The 1/6th Battalion had its headquarters in the town in 1914 and over the early years of that war strong friendships were built with residents which endured for many years after. After the formation of their Old Comrades Association in 1919 they held parades and dinners in the town up to the early 1970s. Plaques to their commanding officer and the enduring friendship between the battalion and the townsfolk were erected, and may still be seen in the parish church of St Nicholas.

The Royal Norfolk Regiment Association (London Branch) on their Annual Cenotaph Parade, 2 June 1957. Over forty members, marshalled by Capt Cozens, attended. The wreath of Flanders poppies was laid by Brig C.J. Wilkinson, Colonel of the Regiment.

The modern embodiment of The Royal Norfolk Regiment is A (Norfolk & Suffolk) Company, 6th (V) Battalion, Royal Anglian Regiment. Pictured is the squad for the 25th Anniversary Freedom Parade, Bury St Edmunds, 31 March 1996. Back row, left to right: Cpl Henderson, Pte Smith, Pte Cowey, Pte Fellen, Pte Price, Sgt Green, Pte Nickalls, Pte Poole, C-Sgt Langley-Stevens, L-Cpl Roe, L-Cpl Palmer, Pte Wiseman, Pte Jones, Pte Boardman, Pte Antill, Pte Hampshire. Front row: L-Cpl Demretser, Pte Nash, Pte Spears, Pte McDonald, Pte Coleman, Sgt Ruchmere, WO2 Debenham, Major Fradley, Capt Chivers, Lt Taylor, Pte Slater, Sgt Fuller, L-Cpl Pollard, L-Cpl Brown.

The final words must go to one of the finest Colonels of The Royal Norfolk Regiment, Gen Sir Ernest Peter Strickland KCB, KBE, CMG, DSO, JP, proud to be a 'Holyboy' to the last, whose farewell speech to the depot and assembled guests at Britannia Barracks on 26 February 1946 summed up his own feelings, and I believe those of many people who served, knew and loved their beloved old county regiment, The Royal Norfolk Regiment – the 9th of Foot. 'You are here this morning representing The Royal Norfolk Regiment as there are no more men available. You have come here for me to say goodbye to you as Colonel of your regiment. I think you will realize with what regret I do it. It is a difficult and unpleasant thing to sever connections with the regiment with which you have been associated for fifty-eight years. Twenty-nine of these years I have been your Colonel. I joined the 2nd Battalion in Mandalay where our 2nd Battalion was fighting. Twenty-seven years ago I was in Mandalay and fighting, and it is nice that it is the same Battalion with which I served when I first joined. Quite a few of you have served in that battalion. I ask you, as all of you serving in your respective battalions to remember the Regiment you serve with keep your pride in it, and keep your associations with it. . . . I shall no longer see officially that badge of which we are so proud and to hear the "Rule Britannia", our March Past. That "Rule Britannia" is looked upon by many regiments in this army with great pride, and they think they have a prior claim to it. They have no prior claim, and I hope that it will remain as long as the Army remains. I also say to you, as I say to all men who are leaving the army, and that is, that all good soldiers (and I take it for granted that you are all good soldiers) make good citizens, so remember when your time comes that you can still serve your King and Country as good citizens as you did in the war.'

ACKNOWLEDGEMENTS

I would like to record my appreciation to the following without whose contributions this book would not have been complete: Captain John Lincoln MC; Terry Davy; Basil Gowen; Philip Standley; Harry Barnard; Bill Loads; Dennis Cross; the Trustees of The Royal Norfolk Regimental Museum; Eastern Counties Newspapers (with special thanks to the staff of the photographic library); the Imperial War Museum; Major Stephen Fradley; Dora Adams and Terry Burchell for the usual photographic wonders.

I would also like to express my sincere thanks for the support of the veterans of The Royal Norfolk Regiment and their families it has been my pleasure and honour to meet over the years. Without exception they have given me ongoing support, encouragement and inspiration; many of them entrusting some of their precious, often irreplaceable, photos and memorabilia in my care for which words cannot express how grateful I am. Without all of them my research, collection and this book simply could not have been possible. I must also record a very special thanks to ex-Colour-Sergeant John Slaughter who encouraged me in my early years of collecting; he has been a constant and authoritative source of information, as well as a good friend.

Finally but by no means least I record my sincere thanks to all my family and special thanks to my darling Sarah for her love and support for this temperamental author.

Every effort has been made in this book to obtain permission to reproduce the photographs herein from their copyright holders but owing to the age of many of the pictures or anonymity of the photographers it has not been possible in every case to trace them, so if any breach of those rights has occurred the author apologises and assures that no offence was intended.

Some of the members of The Royal Norfolk Regiment living history group, 1997. They portray 17 Platoon, D Company 1st Battalion, Royal Norfolk Regiment, c. 1944, at shows, tattoos and displays across Norfolk, Great Britain and at special events in Europe. Through painstaking research and a strong commitment to authenticity and detail they give viewers a valuable insight into the life of the Second World War infantry soldier. Working closely and respectfully with the members of the 1st Battalion Royal Norfolk Regiment D-Day Veterans Association they are acknowledged as one of the foremost living history groups in the country contributing to and featuring in numerous television programmes, magazine articles and books.